D0105439

Schooling _____
the _____
Spirit _____

SCHOOLING THE SPIRIT

Geoffrey Clark

Santa Maria : Asylum Arts : 1993

Acknowledgements

Some of these stories first appeared in the following magazines: *Bachy*, *Mississippi Review*, *The Miscellany*, as well as in two previous collections, *What the Moon Said*, and *Ruffian on the Stair*.

ISBN No. 1-878580-36-1
Library of Congress Catalogue Number 93-72709

Cover photo and design by Greg Boyd.

Contents

for Richard Yates

Schooling the Spirit

Some of these pieces, then, begin in the mire; as if man is no more than a shape writhing from the old rock. This may be due, in part, to the Michigan from which I come. Sometimes one gets the feeling that not even the animals have been there before; but the marsh, the mire, the Void is always there, immediate and terrifying. It is a splendid place for schooling the spirit.

Theodore Roethke, "Open Letter"

I'll leave believing we keep all we lose and love.

Richard Hugo, "Last Day There"

Crazy 8's

Miller Springstead, feet bare, padded expectantly up the hard-packed gravel drive, scarcely glancing to his right at the several acres of jumbled car bodies that constituted the capital of TURNER'S AUTO & TRUCK PARTS. Straight ahead lay the barn and leaning outbuildings, but he turned left, swung back the cedar gate, and walked over the thick cool shag of the Springstead lawn toward their front door—the falling evening had dimmed just enough so he could see the warm glow from electric lights inside. The dew-wet grass was cool under his soles. He was vaguely hungry although he and his father had eaten little more than an hour ago—heavy damp pancakes Turner had made with oatmeal in them to give them a chewy texture.

It occurred to Miller to look for an apple in the kitchen, then seek out Turner in the living room where he'd no doubt be listening to either the CBS or NBC news that came every hour on the hour from New York City. Maybe he could cajole Turner into leaving off with the stupid news and get him out on the back porch where they could sit on their lawn chairs and play Crazy 8's until his older brother Rex got back from the baseball game in Vulcan, where he'd be playing first base for the Ermine Falls Bluejays.

Miller tried to estimate how long that might take, and wondered if the bugs would be bad by the time Rex got back; when they were really swarming, mostly June bugs and moths and flying ants, you could hear them ping against the metal reflector around the porch light and, if you looked up, see them and at the same time feel the silken coolness of the falling dew. Occasionally a bat would skim inside the light's perimeters.

His father had been grouchy and terse the last couple of days, and there were times when, drinking coffee at the dining room table shoved up against the north wall of the living room and

9

listening to every scrap of news from New York on his Hallicrafter's Sky Buddy, Turner's face would darken with something Miller couldn't interpret for sure—it looked like rage at certain times, disgust at others, and sometimes like a response to physical pain.

Miller himself was sick of the news, resentful of it in general because it had seemed to become an obsession rather than a pastime for Turner.

"...four thousand dollars for an escape to Mexico," he heard the radio announcer say as he paused on the doorstep.

"...David Greenglass...twice the Vatican sent word the Pope had received urgent appeals..."

Damned commie bastard spies, Miller thought: Serves 'em goddamn right.

"...President Eisenhower refused a last request for executive clemency..."

Miller opened the screen door and stepped in. Turner was to his left and bent low in his chair, almost crouching toward his Sky Buddy: "The long wait is over. Tonight, less than five minutes ago, an electrician ended the lives of Ethel and Julius Rosenberg in the death house at Sing-Sing for a fee of three hundred dollars. The double execution, in which Julius died first, his wife ten minutes later, ended more than two years of legal maneuvering and world-wide agitation for commutation of the death sentence. Twenty-six months elapsed between conviction and execution during which the defense raised more than twenty points of law in petitions and writs and sent more than three appeals to the White—"

Turner twisted a knob of the radio so hard it came off in his hand. He looked at it for a moment with loathing, then, still seated, hurled it against the wall, where it created a divot—a bit of mouse-gray lathing peeped through the broken plaster.

"Pa, what the hell..."

Turner turned toward his son, his face contorted. In a low growl that made Miller think of stones grinding against the wall of a cement mixer, he said: "Goddamnit all to fucking hell."

"What?" Just behind Miller's knees were points of pure powerlessness.

As if in reasonable answer to his son's question, Turner said in the same stone-grinding growl: "Goddamned-son-of-a-bitching-whore-mongering-monkey-fucking-pissy-assed-shitface-son-of-a-pig-fucking-low-life-whore."

He paused, and slowly drew in a deep fresh breath.

Miller had backed unconsciously toward the door, yet he stuck in the doorframe, half-frightened, yet curious, too, to see if his old man might create even more stupendous curses.

But Turner's next words were entirely literal, devoid of the pith and fur of connotation: "That's one reason why you're going to college, pal, so you ain't reduced to god-damning and son-of-a-bitching it. Christamighty! We ain't learned nothing, we ain't even come close...'course, what the hell do you expect out of a country mostly put together out of the dregs and scum of Europe, no matter what they teach you to school. And why not? Jesus H. Christ, you empty out the pokies and debtors' prisons, scrape the gutters for cut-throat trash, get you all the religious loons and hunters and trappers and general assholes banded together...and, then you turn'em all loose on an innocent continent—ever wonder how this country must have been before it got all fucked up?"

Pictures of Ellis Island, the phrase "melting pot," the image of the Statue of Liberty whizzed into Miller's mind like bats: then the phrase "the winning of the West" seemed to circulate and eddy in his mind's eye, as if on a banner pulled by a small airplane.

"But Pa," Miller whispered, "they was communists—spies!" He was incapable of grappling with anything more complex in the face of Turner's curious wrath or scorn or whatever it was. More phrases from his high school history book which his father knew better than he did filled the space where the twisting banner reading The Winning of the West had fluttered: Plymouth Rock. Bunker Hill. Fifty-Four-Forty-or-Fight. Tippicanoe and Tyler too! Fire when you see the whites of their eyes. Damn the torpedoes and full speed ahead. I only regret that I have but one life to give to my country. If this be treason, let us make the most of it. A stitch in time saves nine.

Turner's eyes cooled rapidly, and he ran a hand around the thick nappy curled silver hair above his ears and at the back of his scalp, scratching and massaging, exasperated with himself, his fit spent: "What the hell," he said gently, "I expect the old U S of A maybe ain't so bad...better'n any other, that's for sure...well,

11

anyways, pal, I don't know much, but I do know the word is the key to things, and I don't want to see you end up like your old man with nothing but a pack of cusswords to trot out as wherewithal when the shit hits the fan..."

Turner got up from the chair ponderously, almost decrepitly, as if he'd sat still for too long after heavy work and had let himself get stiff. Slowly he bent over and picked up the black knob from the radio which had come to rest a few feet from his chair. It lay in his open palm and he regarded it curiously.

"Aw, come on, you ain't all *that* bad," Miller told him seriously, knowing his own eyes must be round and wide with something like wonder.

Turner rolled the black knob around slowly in his palm, and when he looked up at last he was smiling. "Why, thank you, pal."

Miller regarded his father intently, minutely, but as near as he could tell, Turner did not seem to be kidding.

Lunar Frisson

Rex Springstead lolls in the tub at home. He is seventeen, mature and lean and finely made, adroit-looking even naked.

His fourteen year-old brother, Miller, is in the can with him.

Their father, Turner, is downstairs listening to the radio, addicted as he is to continuous news from CBS in New York.

Miller, shoeless, in jeans and T-shirt, sits on the stool's closed lid, dreaming of 1957 when he will be seventeen and, like Rex, will have him a Ford coupe (a Merc would also do). And when he's around sixteen he thinks he'll probably buy his own razor and brush and, like Rex, use Turner's shaving mug on the sly and though Turner will know this, nothing will ever be said, as if there'd all along been some kind of agreement things would work out like this.

Miller is about five-seven, three inches shorter than Rex, and is blond and stocky, muscles already swollen from heavy work in the junkyard and from lifting weights.

"If that osmosis bullshit in biology worked through wood, Miller, just think—you could drop a load in the commode setting right where you are," Rex says, soaping a foot.

"Your ass sucks canal water," Miller says, an idiom he's heard a few times; he hopes to sound tough, strong, bored, mature.

Rex snickers, slops water lovingly around his parts, crooning to them as though they are little animals. "There you go, little pals, you'll be all scrubbed up and smelling sweet as toilet water. Never can tell what a feller like me's liable to run into at a free show...if I run into something familiar, I expect I'll probably just have to fuck'er again..."

He winks at Miller, who glowers and then speaks with the grainy truculence of adolescence: "A-*gain*, huh?"

It is a Friday evening, late June, there's a free show tonight in Ermine Falls.

Rex stretches out in the stubby, archaic tub, his long, finely muscled legs with their skeins of lustrous dark hair arching like birds' wings out over the tub's rim, his eyes shut. So voluptuous is his involvement with himself that Miller half-sighs with envy.

Rex cocks one eye open, offers a lazy grin: "Why shit yes, again a table, again a car, again a tree, I take it where I can get it. Tell you, old buddy, I believe tonight I'd put the blocks to a snake if somebody'd hold its head."

Rex reaches for the sliver of Lifebuoy in the wire soap dish next to the Lava. Miller has often wondered why, using first gasoline, then waterless soap, then Lava, then Lifebuoy, he can never quite get all the ingrained grease from the grooves and whorls of his fingerprints, nor under his nails, while Rex usually can.

When Rex stands before the mirror in his shorts working his brush against the soap in Turner's mug, Miller asks: "Hey, Rex...'sposin' I was to come across a little nookie myself tonight, y'never know, you got any hot tips on a sure-fire way to get laid...if I should just happen to fall over some likely quiff, that is..."

Hearing his own voice crack a little around the edges, Miller awaits the tart rejoinder he anticipates: *Better wait'll you're a little more growed up and got some hair on your ass, fuzznuts, before you...*

But instead: "Hmmmmmph..." Rex builds up lather in the mug, then spreads it on his face. New soapy odors augment the scent of Lifebuoy. "First thing," Rex says softly, "you got to get her hot, see..."

The hackles on Miller's neck rise and his jaw slackens a bit.

"Trapping flies?"

Miller shuts his mouth.

"Okay, Miller, tell you what, let's us reckon you're to the free show tonight, and say you got a kind of a date with...say, cute little Ruth Ann Perkins."

Miller's groin buzzes a little: Ruth Ann Perkins: small, but mature for thirteen, little button eyes, quick like a Banty hen, hard little tits, an ass whose each little buttock looks as delicately sculpted as the bowl of an antique sugar spoon...the vision makes his mouth go dry and his parts tingle.

Rex's voice, theatrically lowered, runs on with damp sugges-

14

tion: "...so let's us say you'n her are on your blanket and you're watching the show—it ain't much good, but you set there with your Royal Crown Cola and peanuts and you're holding her hand...whyn't you put the whole bag of peanuts down the neck of your RC, that'll free up your other hand a bit..."

Rex grins into the mirror, and his white desert rat's beard of lather bends to its configuration, giving him a canny, almost sly look: "...after a time you work an arm around her and you sniff her hair—smells kind of like vanilla and lemon squeezings and new hay...makes it kind of hard for you to swallow, don't it?"

Miller gulps as throat and pecker thicken.

"...next thing you know, like she kind of knew it all along, you both get up and you both kind of slink off—now, it's important to goddamn *slink*, see, that gives it all just the right spice. So you keep aholt of her little hand all the while and take the blanket and just sidle away from the doings—if the holy rollers come out from the Bi-Way Gospel Tabernacle and come down to sing and carry on and try to drown out the fucking heathen show, why that's even better, Christ yes, then *everybody's* watching or cussing them and there ain't nobody but the big old moon to watch you'n her scurry off..."

Miller croaks a feeble objection: "But Ruth Ann's folks go to the Tabernacle now, they'd likely be keeping an eye on her no matter if they was there singing or not..."

"Aaaahh—" Rex dismisses the possibility with a wave of one hand before he pulls the little waxen paper away from a new Gilette Blue Blade and fits it into his safety razor: "Like I say, that just adds a little more spice—sneaking around is always good for loving, especially when there's Christers mixed up in it somehow. So let's us just say her folks have come down with the rest of the Christers and they're standing there howling away beside the projection booth." He gestures with his razor and begins to sing,

"We are sinking
Deep in sin,"

then after a brief pause hollers out, hard enough so he nicks his Adam's Apple: "*Wheeee!*"

"Shit, now lookit, god-damnit, I'm bleeding like a stuck hog..."

15

Dry-mouthed, Miller silently hands him a wad of toilet paper: *Yeah? Yeah? And then?*

"...so say you go along hand-in-hand in the moonlight, she's a full one tonight, ain't she?...you maybe walk her over by the school, maybe she sets in a swing and you push her for a bit, touching her every chance you get, I mean you push right below the small of her back so you're just only barely touching the tops of both cheeks of her cute little ass...well, one time when her swing comes back, you don't give her a push, see, instead you wrap your arms around her, you bury your nose in that sweet-smelling hair... you skootch your face between her neck and her shoulder—hey, you listening? You okay? You look a little white around the gills, there, palzie-walzie..."

Miller whispers hoarsely, "It'll pass."

"Mmmmm..." Rex finishes off the underside of his throat and runs his fingers along it for vagrant stubble. He rinses his razor and goes to his sideburns, stretching the skin of his jaw taut: "She turns her face around and you take it gentle in your hands and you plant one on her—now here's where you got to do her just right"—Rex hefts the dripping razor for emphasis—"not too much, nor not too little...so you start working on your French kiss, know what I mean?"

Miller swallows, nods, forgetting to breathe.

"Give'er the old tongue," Rex suggests moistly, "but easy: you don't want to go whole hog on your early stuff, that's the ticket, see, you'll catch on just fine. If she gives you a little tongue back, why, then, know what they say, if some's good, more's better. If she don't, why then, go back to where you was and start working up all over again, only be gentler this time, right?"

"Yeah," Miller breathes. There is a sand burr buried somewhere deep inside his groin.

"...and pretty soon you take her over behind the giants and swings—you know just there t'other side of the west corner of the ball diamond, there where the woods begins, where there ain't too much nor too little cover? Stay over away from the dugouts. Now remember, there's a big full moon'n it just lights things up nice and romantic, right?"

"Yeah..."

"So you spread your blanket out and you two lay down together...and you draw her up close so's you can breathe in her

16

ear, then—this's important, now—you take her ear real gentle between your lips—try to keep your teeth out of the way—and you give'er some little ear bites with just your lips, drives'em fucking crazy every time...then..."

Rex is staring into the mirror, razor no longer poised but dangling slackly between thumb and forefinger. "Then you kiss her on the neck, and in all the soft hollow places you can find, you run your hand up under her shirt—Ruth Ann's likely got jeans on, ain't she? That could be a problem: tight jeans're a problem sometimes..."

Miller realizes what the new note in his brother's voice means: he is taking possession of Miller's own warmly churning Ruth Ann, shouldering his brother aside: *Hey*, Miller feels like saying, *just a goddamn minute here!*

"...now you got the top button of her jeans undone, now you got to be kissing her all the time and be touching her firm but easy as you work your hand downwards—a woman appreciates your being gentle, but she don't want too much shilly-shallying around either. Besides, you go and be *too* delicate, maybe you'll tickle her, nothing worse'n making her giggle, at least in the early part—cutting a fart when you get to humping, maybe—but anyhow now you've got her bra unhooked, them hooks can be something else, can't they, and now you've had your lips on them hard little titties, whew, Ruth Ann's're *real* nice even if they are a trifle small...now, then, when you put the tip of your tongue in her ear, touch it in a few different places, and give'er some sweet nothings for good measure: 'Oh, Ruth Ann, honey, your skin's smoother'n glass, you're sweeter'n honey'—that kind of crap. Just be *god*damn sure you don't tell her you love her no matter what, or you'll end up engaged or something and you won't know whether to go shit or go blind. Remind me 'fore I leave and I'll lend you a rubber."

"I ain't old enough to get married, and I don't ever plan on it anyhow," Miller says with as much haughtiness as he can muster. "If getting married was worth a shit, Turner would probably of got married again."

"Age don't mean shit around these parts," Rex counsels blandly, eyes dreamy, still turned inward upon the tableau of seduction he has created. "Anyhow, when she starts to give these little whimpers or whines, it may be that whether she gives you a Yes or a No don't matter much, she means Yes...your finger dips kind of gentle but firm into her tight little pussy, it's wet now and you work *reeel* slow up towards the top..."

"Yeah..."

And Miller is with his humid Ruth Ann beneath the gelid moon, their clothes are getting off, their jeans three-quarters down, they are vessels of simmering liquid desire as all about them green things yield their scents to the night—

"Your hand's come up a little now, you start to push, don't pull—her jeans'll come all the way down just fine if you're careful, you just keep petting and kissing and touching her, touching that top part of her pussy that's slick and that makes her whine a little more...then you work your other arm and push your drawers down, you take her sweaty little hand and put it right onto your old dong..."

Rex's voice falters, his eyes slowly focus on his half-lathered face in the mirror. He brings the razor to his throat and takes an awkward upward stroke: "Damn! Cut myself again!"

But then he studies the blood on his fingertips with bemusement rather than irritation: "Let that be a lesson to you, horniness makes you careless, and it's just like they say, a stiff prick's got no—Jesus Christ, Miller!"

Miller sits on the stool, fingers battened around the lid, blood drumming in his ears, eyes glazed.

"Christalmighty, Miller, I don't expect I'd try to blink my eyes none if I was you, you'll bust a gusset somewhere..."

As Miller's eyes come into focus and he regards the mirth standing in pools in his brother's eyes, he licks his dry lips and whispers, "What the fuck..."

"I said, don't blink none because as any fool can plainly see...*you ain't got enough skin left! Haw!*"

And Rex is off into gales of rich guffaws, pointing at Miller's crotch, where sure enough his jeans tent out urgently: "You got what they call a rise in the *Le*-vi's—just goes to show you old Rex, he knows where the bear shit in the buckwheat, that's no lie..."

Rex seems immersed in his joke, but as he turns and pushes some soap from his lips, his fingers tremble. A spot of his blood is bright against the stark white porcelain of the sink.

Scarcely realizing he is in motion, Miller rises from the toilet, awkward with his hard-on, and from the sink he seizes the

18

sodden washcloth Rex is intending to use to remove the last traces of lather.

Miller pulls back the waistband of Rex's Fruit of the Looms and drops the soppy mess warm as piss into his brother's crotch, then slams from the tiny humid room and lurches into the cool spaciousness of the living room.

Though it is scarcely seven o'clock, Miller can already see the rising full moon through the living room windows, and for some reason he recalls a burl of purplish varicose veins like a vegetable growth he once saw on the forearm of a truck driver.

Miller Springstead watches the the moon until it jigs to the pounding of his heart.

Blood Blossom

Turner is touchier about it than a teen-ager with a troublesome pimple, and he keeps testing it around the edges when he thinks I'm not watching.

"Hell, why wait, why not just try to get hold of the end of the thread with your fingers like you would for a splinter? It ain't going to hurt no matter what, is it?" I ask.

"No, you can't hardly consider anything I might do to this thing hurt and it's sure not doing me any harm. Funny, I thought the one two years ago was probably the last, but no matter what, you just can't seem to rub the damned war off like it was soot."

"Well, if you just pull the whole damn thing off, you're bound to get that little thing of thread too, ain't you?"

He snorts mirthlessly. "That's a teen-ager's solution. No, it'd probably disappear back into me like a snake going back in his hole. I want it to work its way out natural and fall on the ground like a piece of rotten fruit...you got to outsmart it, seems to me..."

I consider this. It is mid-August of 1957 and Turner and I sit in the shade of the single huge leafy maple in the center of the four acres or so of junked cars and farm machinery and trucks from which we make our living—I am counting on this yard to see me through college a little later on.

I sit on a rump-sprung front seat pulled from a 48 Chevy and put under the tree; Turner sits shirtless on a patch of shaded grass to my left. It must be close to 90 in the shade, and the maple leaves are wilted.

Slyly, I study Turner, admiring the shrapnel scars in relief on his back and the odd sunken L-shaped wound on his left forearm made by a Japanese bayonet some 15 years before.

It's hard not to keep looking back to the shiny blood blossom about half the size of a dime on his left pectoral: it's like a big drop of purple rain kept brilliant, whole and symmetrical by surface tension. The slab of muscle to which it clings is covered with grizzled hair—the same half-black, half-gray hair that grows in thick curly patches around the scars on his back. Turner is broad and powerful and his arm working a chain pull when we pull an engine is an anatomy lesson; nor is there any lazy droop or sag to his belly as with most men in their forties; his abdominal muscles ripple under skin that's loose and a bit wrinkled, as if he lost a bit of weight once and never gained it back.

There's also a scar you can't see that runs up the inside of his right thigh, and one shaped like a check mark that runs from his lower belly down into his pubic hair.

All these wounds save the forearm one, Turner once told me, were stitched together in a Marine Corps field hospital in the South Pacific with suture material designed to never be removed: after a time the stuff was supposed to melt away, leaving no trace of itself...but, it was explained to Turner a few years after the war at the VA hospital in Grand Rapids, the stuff didn't always dissolve: sometimes bits of it remained, little filaments, Sputniks of the blood traveling through their host's circulatory system until, with the right combination of temperature, labor and sweat, they'd begin to nudge up against the bulkheads of blood vessels like fish in a live box, and finally one would begin to work its way out with a razory little nose, announcing itself as a burning little pustule of blood and lymph.

Turner explained his method of dealing with them when he had the last one two years ago: you wait until you see the minutest bit of filament protruding from the blood blossom and you capture it very delicately with a pair of tweezers and pull it carefully from its sanguine dome—and then let it fall to the ground and join the dust and milkweed fluff blowing back and forth across the land TURNER'S AUTO & TRUCK PARTS sits on.

I keep my eyes off Turner for a time. We are finishing sandwiches I made this morning, fried pork and cheese and spinach greens and mayonnaise. I am grateful for the shade of the huge drooping maple. Sometimes bundles of light seem to fly from hunks of chromed metal in the yard about us and into your eyes like something winged.

The smells of gasoline, grease, and empty car interiors that have baked in the sun for years surround us. The yard may appear nearly lifeless, but beneath the jumble of metal and encroaching vegetation there is life aplenty—garter and milk snakes in profusion, gophers, field mice, ground hogs...even now bugs and roaches are probably swimming delightedly through batting from ripped upholstery popped into static waterfalls.

Our sandwiches finished, we suck on Nehi root beers plucked from a dripping aluminum pot of long-melted ice.

We digest and rest up. We have finished stripping down an old five-ton International truck, and now the transmission and rear end rest on the wagon behind the tractor. All we have to do now is haul the stuff back to the shop and have it ready to put on our customer's truck—we have an order for both pieces.

Rex is minding the shop, and I know when we get back Turner'll give us the rest of the day off to go swimming. Rex is leaving for the Army next month and Turner's taking it pretty easy on both of us right now.

We sweat though we're out of the sun and at rest, and I feel parched, dehydrated, in spite of all the water I've drunk earlier, and the pop with lunch. To make conversation and to offer Turner an opportunity to keep away from the topic of the blood blossom I say, "Damned heat's a corker, ain't it? Don't it make you want to be in Alaska or someplace, anywhere but here?"

Turner's pale blue eyes, empty as he'd chewed his sandwich, fill with sudden attention, and he looks at me as if I've asked him something difficult. He thinks for a few moments, then says "Why, no, no, it don't."

When he says nothing more, I prod him a little: "Aw, come on, Turner, if you had your druthers, wouldn't you rather be—"

"I'd sooner be here than anywhere...good Christ, being out sweating on your own land's a privilege." He gives me a serious, canny, merchant's kind of look: "I love the junk business. It was made for an old bottom feeder like me. Hell, you get you a decent late model wreck to auction, then sell her off piece by piece, and if you ain't impatient, wellsir, before you know it you've turned a real decent profit. And because it's so slow and dumb-looking, ain't nobody really much envying you..." Turner's voice trails off, a cloudiness fills his eyes, a grimace passes over his face.

I recognize the signs: most times you can't get a straight answer to a straight question about the war from Turner, but then sometimes out of nowhere comes a piece of it—

22

"Any sweat ain't fear-sweat's okay with me," Turner says slowly, as if to someone else.

"Fear-sweat?"

I think at first Turner hasn't heard me it takes him so long to answer. But then he says, "Once I was at a place called Henderson Field on Guadalcanal during the war and I remember one day in 1942 when for a whole goddamned Sunday we was in holes in the ground, hiding under palm logs and metal junk, hell, anything we could lay our hands on that could cover us. And the Japs came over us all day, in the rain, bombing the living shit out of us. The field was a quagmire and half-bombed out, with a few broken down dive bombers, Avengers they was, on it. It was like the whole world was bombs and rain. And sweat. Then when the bombing quit, they was hand-to-hand, with the Japs coming at you like bugs out of the woodwork...well, just before your hand-to-hand, that's when what was coming out of your pores was fear-sweat, you can tell it because it's ice-fucking-cold, and it seems like your heart and balls is flowing out with it..."

"You must of killed a bunch of Japs in the war, huh, Pa?"

I am excited, yet don't want to spook Turner or let him know how much I admire, hell, envy him—though I am old as seventeen, as early as yesterday I was dreamily reading a war comic somebody'd left in the shop, *Heroic Hall of Honor*, stories of heroism from World War ll to Korea—there were six instances of brave GIs doing noble deeds, local boys like me polishing off the Japs, the Krauts, the Gooks; I could easily insert myself into the situation, carrying a wounded buddy through skeins of deadly small-arms fire, or leaping on a fizzing grenade to save my pals. Or myself, an artillery observer so Gung-Ho he leaves his post to lead a charge into Gook trenches...*Near Tumil-li the Second Infantry Division was engaged in a fierce battle with a fanatical enemy force...Sgt. Miller Springstead was in the thick of it...*

But Turner doesn't like references to the war, his or Korea (though he listens avidly a dozen times a day and sometimes far into the night to his Hallicrafter's Sky Buddy, getting news on the hour from either NBC or CBS in New York City), will not see a war movie. And on the rare occasions I'd heard him talk to another serviceman who'd been in the South Pacific, eavesdropping had proven disappointing: only discussion of places,

23

dates, weather, and action only in the collective sense, never in the personal.

For almost a minute Turner says nothing, looking off at the twisted car bodies around us. And when he does speak, his voice is thick—does he know he's talking to me?

"Yeah. Yeah. Yeah, I did, I killed me a goodly batch of Japs, me'n others...fact is, we more or less exterminated a lot of the little buggers like they was lice...or gophers..."

"How?" I say carefully, restraining my eagerness, knowing I can stampede him into silence if I'm not careful.

But Turner seems far away, and answering somebody else's question: "Was a time I was the bloodthirstiest sonofabitch you could imagine—you had to be to be a good Marine. I was in the Second Marines that took a place called Tarawa..God, shit, all them names..Makin, Bougainville, Arawe, they're bitter names..."

I do not nod, but frown stonily, maturely, at the ground and whip the root beer in my bottle to a froth. I don't spit, though I feel like it.

"We went in and took an island named Betio, in on LSTs through so goddamned many barbed wire and cement obstacles you couldn't imagine. Oh, they'd done a good job, the Nips was experts. We was getting it from shore from machine guns and mortars, all hid. There was pillboxes all around the island, even some medium tanks. Our air support hit so much fire they wasn't worth shit, but in we goddamn went. Took about five days to take Betio and when she was took...there was thousands of stiffs all over, Marines and Japs, in every cranny, dead Marines hanging from the barbwire obstacles... the beach was such a fucking litter of death you couldn't describe her without comparing her to hell. They wasn't hardly nothing left standing except the goddamn cement and steel and palm log pillboxes. Me, I helped take some of them pillboxes with enough craziness and rage as to make a Samurai cry with envy..."

Pride swells my bare chest as I see him in the thick of combat, a fine muscular Marine with tattered netting on his helmet, advancing through the fire and brimstone of battle at the head of a platoon, bullets whizzing past his head as he dauntlessly hurls hand grenades with one hand and blazes away with his .45 automatic in the other.

"How did you take them, Turner?"

24

"Mainly we cooked them." Turner's jaw muscles go rigid.

"What do you mean?"

"I mean I run a flame thrower. I used to burn the Nips out of pillboxes. I'd get me some decent cover fire and get close and burn the bastards out through the gun slits and apertures. Then later, after we'd took Betio, I was in charge of a mop-up squad, we'd go around and get the left-over Nips hiding in holes and caves..."

"How'd you—"

"When we run out of jellied gas for the throwers, and we was short on things like TNT and grenades, we used plain old gasoline to burn'em out...and you know, for the longest time, something in me loved the war, goddamn loved it. Everything was clean-cut, you knew who you was for and who you was against. And I hated the Japs for all the usual reasons..."

Yes, I consider saying, me too, and Rex, we hated the Japs. I remember them cartoons of Tojo with his big front teeth, and when you was at the war me'n Rex used to pick milkweed pods like they made life jackets out of and sell'em to Guilder's for fifty cents a bag to buy war bonds with...

"Oh, Christalmighty how I hated the Japs, made me feel my nuts was the size of coconuts. Sometimes when they'd come screaming out of holes in the ground on fire and take off running, we wouldn't even waste a round to polish'em off with. I used to think, You little yellow sonsofbitches, kill my buddies, will you, try to take over my country, well, I ain't forgot Pearl Harbor, oh, something in me jumped for joy there was a war, I must've killed Christ knows how many Japs by blasting or burning, though I only killed one face to face...it was a buddy shot him that stuck a bayonet through my arm..."

There is no longer any need to worry about him finishing, for he is hooked on his own narrative.

He leans forward a bit, hands tightening on his quarter-full bottle of warm root beer. "Miller, once upon a time me'n a corporal named Woods was in such jungle as there was more or less on our own hook, on the lookout for stray Nips, scouting holes, tunnels, caves, anything. Nips was geniuses at hiding. Anyhow, we run smack into a wounded Jap officer, laying there on the jungle floor, panting, don't know where the hell he thought he could get to. His one leg was like to blasted off at the knee, but he'd got a tourniquet on it. Well, to make it short, we

25

had the drop on him. We figured we'd better take him in since he was an officer..."

Turner swallows absently, brings the root beer to his lips, but then lets it dangle untasted. His blood blossom seems to wax in a tear-shaped bit of sunlight that has found it out, shiny as a new dime.

"To make it short, Woods got a little over-eager to get this Samurai sword the Jap had and he got careless. Me, I never went in much for souvenirs, nor ever dug the gold out of dead Japs' teeth with my bayonet the way some did. Anyhow, I covered the Jap with my carbine, but then somehow Woods got between me'n the Jap and when he was tugging on that sword, the Jap somehow twisted around quicker'n shit and hauled out a Nambu—Jap pistol—and shot Woods dead center in the chest, he must of been dead before he hit the ground, still holding the sword...well, I went storming over and before the Jap could take a crack at me I kicked him hard as I could under the chin, shoved his lower jaw half off his face and sent him ass-over-teakettle...and when he tried to raise himself up again, I kicked him in the mouth—I'd seen soldiers and Marines and even one Seabee and what the Japs'd done, beat them horrible, tortured them, cut off their balls and shoved them in their mouths...once I seen six Marines with their heads laying on the sand in front of their bodies on a beach prettier'n anything on Silverfish Lake.

"Anyhow, before I knew it, I'd ripped that sword out of Woods' dead hand and went for the Jap. He seen me coming, he looked at me once coming for him and I looked into his eyes. He hunched a little forward and bent his head down for me to lop her off. His arms was shaking from holding that position as I come up to him...and kicked him again, into a setting-up position, and then I lifted that heavy sharp sword like it was an axe and I come down on the top of his head like he was a chunk of oak. I split him in half... And then I puked. Not from the blood and guts, you understand, I'd seen so much that didn't affect me, but I seen for the first time he was just a man same as me and for a second it seemed like I was there on the jungle floor, split down the middle.

"And suddenly I thought about you and Rex for the first time in months. And I thought, Jesus Christ, suppose the war don't kill me like I always figured it would: what if I go back? What if somehow I come out of all this alive?

26

"Something in me started shrinking...don't get me wrong, I shot off plenty more guns before I was through, and I'd of killed to protect myself or my buddies—or my boys, or even my dog—and still would. But somehow, far as I know, nothing has happened since that day where I killed anything...and that's one of the things I lay in fear of in the small hours, that I will one day again be responsible for somebody dying..."

Turner's voice has trailed off, and our eyes lift simultaneously to the glittering tangle of mangled cars where we have grunted and sweated and strained all morning; I shiver, almost queasy with pride in my father...but he has risen quickly and nipped around on the other side of the tree where I hear him puking. But even my concern for him cannot shake my sense of pride, exultation, admiration: *My Pa...*

In a moment Turner returns, cheerful, normal-looking, wiping his face with his balled-up shirt, saying, "You must of put some sour mayonnaise on that sandwich, pal, or else it's too rich for my blood." He looks quickly at the sun to gauge the time. "You think that's a little strange, listen to this." He is grinning idiotically, as if he has been somehow exhilarated by puking. "I hadn't been back in Ermine Falls more'n two weeks and I was looking at this place. I done me some dickering with the VA people and the bank people, and I was driving over here to look this place over again. It was raining. I come along the Plum Valley Road and there was a dead raccoon by the side of the road, feet up, been hit by a car, mouth open, rained on, ugliest and commonest thing imaginable. I stopped the car—39 Packard straight-8—and got out and looked close at it...and collapsed in tears. Me. Big tough Gyrene, bawled like a baby because somehow it was the saddest thing I'd ever seen, me, who'd wandered through Nip stiffs stacked up like cordwood, bloated, their heads tore up for the gold in their teeth...something'd happened and I didn't know what it was, but I figured hell, maybe I wasn't as screwed up as I'd thought. I felt washed clean, but weak, weak's a baby, not necessarily in the muscles but in the spirit...

"I knew then I needed this particular place worse'n I'd ever needed anything—and now it's all these years later and I got her and here we are, and here in this little corner of the world we don't shoot birds, we don't butcher the cow when she don't give milk no more, we don't trap out the skunks." He shakes his head

27

and wipes his gleaming brow with his forearm, moving the sweat around a little.

Suddenly he looks directly into my face to see how I am taking all this—and I guess he must see reverence, admiration, even envy. My eyes leave his and travel again to the marvelous blood blossom.

When I look back at his eyes, I am staggered: are they, can they be, filled with rage?

His head droops and he looks directly upon the red button on his chest. "Now you see it, now you don't," he says sourly; and deliberately, as one might kill a potato bug, his thumb and forefinger descend and tighten caliper-like upon the pustule, a claret sunburst flares around his fingers and dribbles down his belly, staining the waistband of his undershorts, just visible above his belt, purple.

Boozing

Rex came home for Christmas on his first leave from the Army in 1957, when I was going on eighteen and he was twenty. In the four months he'd been away he seemed to've aged two or three years, and at first he seemed a little alien. I watched from his idling 46 Ford coupe which I'd started up and run a little once a week all the time he'd been gone as he strode confidently into Perkin's Drugstore and Package Liquor in Vulcan in his uniform like he'd just got back from defending the U S of A in some desperate encounters against the Hun; through the car and drugstore windows I could see him demand and get four bottles of CVC muscatel. Clearly the old prunefaced bat behind the counter wouldn't have dreamed of asking a sterling young warrior like himself for ID.

We got rolling in his coupe and we had a few belts. And then it seemed to take little more than fifteen minutes before we were drunk as skunks. Rex was gabbling on about how lucky he was to've got a job driving officers around, a real soft touch; then I got to jabbering on about how much I'd been lifting weights—"Shit, Rex, I'm gettin so fuckin' strong I probably got muscle in my shit—"

We drank and drove, drove and drank, all over our old stomping grounds, over to Traverse and back, through Ermine Falls, on to Vulcan and Mancelona, keeping to dirt roads as much as we could, gossiping crazily: "Hey, Rex, I hear tell Sally Bergdorf got knocked up by this guy name of Holt over to Traverse, an' when'er old man found out, he was gonna kill Holt—until he'd found out this Holt'd started his own radio and TV repair, and old man Bergdorf told Howie Yates, 'Godddamn, at last I can get my TV fixed whenever I need it, and for fuckin' *free!*'"

Then suddenly Rex was really drunk out of his mind as we

were heading back to Ermine Falls from Mancelona. We made it okay until about two miles from our place on Highway 31 when Rex got to paying less and less attention to the road and was hollering, "Fuck the Army! Eff Tee-A, thass th' way we say'er..." And on and on about how he hated the Army and loved it at the same time and about all the pussy he was getting. His face above the collar of his uniform turned bright pink: "There's this here cute little blonde like a cheerleader to the whorehouse 'bout two miles from the base who don't let nobody fuck her, nobody atall, ain't that something! Know what she is, Miller, she's table pussy is what the rebel sojers call her, I mean them fuckers'd beat the shit out of any sojer tries to fuck her, they say—oh, aha, guh-guh-goddamn—they say, Don't fuck up the eatin' eat up the fuckin! *Whah!*"

He swung one arm wide back and hit me in the chest and we both started laughing hysterically, and when I looked through the windshield I noticed we were driving ahead into pure white: we drifted over into a ditch full of snow gentle as a falling feather and there we was. When at last I got my laughing under control, I poked Rex in the ribs and said, "Hey, asshole, what we gonna do now?"

But Rex was out cold, already snoring away, with a half-empty bottle of muscatel between his legs, leaking onto his uniform pants.

The next time I looked up it had gotten dark and there was Pop Murkle's car across from us on the road with its red light going and I could see ERMINE FALLS CONSTABLE on the car door. He was coming cautiously down the bank toward us, looked official as hell with his trooper's cap and nylon jacket and badge but I knew the old fart could barely blow his nose without assistance. He came gimping slowly over to us, flashing his light into the car. I rolled the window down and heard gibberish sputtering on the police radio in his car and then Pop was at my window, shining his light in, saying, "Well, looky here, if it ain't the Springstead boys, run smack-ass into the ditch, drunker'n pissants, the two of 'em..."

*

Miller, silent, kept his aching eyes—the sockets felt lined

with ground glass—away from the light over the table and lapped delicately at his black coffee, bringing his face down to the cup rather than trying to hold it. His drunkenness was diminishing, but he continued to crouch behind bogus stupefaction as much as he could to defer though not elude Turner's judgment.

He chanced a glance at Turner as he reached for the ash-filled brass spitoon under the table; the swaying light over the table gave the whorls and kinky configurations of the silver hair gripping the sides of his father's skull the look of feathery hands.

Turner's voice wasn't necessarily sure of itself, but nonetheless it moved forward with a continuity superior to its pauses, digressions or expletives: "...and I reckon you don't remember your mother as nothing but a blur. Probably just as well, hell, I can't bring myself even after all these years to be fair to her. I still tend to think the best woman there is is a bitch. I knew about LaVern when I married her in thirty-seven, two months after I knocked her up with Rex. I reckon she was still a bitch when she pulled out in forty with a truck farmer from Rome, Georgia, who'd got into her while she was waitressing to White's in town. Like I say, I ain't seen her in going on seventeen years, when she left me flat—and me, *me*, I'd of done the same goddamn thing had I been her. 'Cause whatever I may be now, I'm a fucking-A prince compared with the Turner Springstead of them days. For one thing, I used to be a boozer on such a Christawful scale you prob'ly wouldn't recognize that Turner Springstead if he rose up out of the past and bit you on the ass—which is something he might've done. I mean I wasn't fit to be lived around, let alone with. And as for you and Rex, that was just another goddamn trick on me...

"But here's the short of it on how come I don't drink now. One morning in late forty I woke up after this binge I'd throwed just after I'd joined the Corps—figured I'd get drafted anyhow, so I thought I might's eliminate the middleman and go right into the Corps. I woke up with the grandaddy of all hangovers, weak's a cat, could hardly hold up my head to pour a morning beer in it after I'd throwed up once...I dragged myself into the kitchen of this little shithook rented house with no running water except for a pitcher pump in the kitchen. I was making reasonable money then, working to the Ford garage in Skeegemog, but we wasn't living very high on the hog, what with two kids and my boozing and LaVern, who could spend it pretty good in them days. So like I say, I got my ass into the kitchen and here was this note: 'Going back south and never coming back. LaVern S.' Just about that time you'd got out of the playpen in the extra bedroom and come crawling into the kitchen with your diaper full of shit, howling at the top of your lungs. Rex was staying to Sonney and Pearl's that day. Anyhow, I picked you up and ripped your diaper off and slung it against a wall. Then I hefted this wriggling little shit-smeared tadpole named Miller, held him up by his heels like he was a rabbit I'd just dressed out, and I started to work the pitcher pump. Bastard wouldn't go until I primed her with some stale beer—and then I pumped a stream of ice-cold water over your baby's ass, water so cold I couldn't hold my hand under it for long. You hollered louder and louder until I could hardly stand it...

"Somehow I got you wrapped in an old pair of my drawers and got you into a little pair of overalls LaVern'd got you and I took you over to Sonney and Pearl's. I give Sonney ten bucks and left him there with you, shaking his head. I was off again.

"I got me in a goodly supply of booze and laid me down there in that little crackerbox of a house. It was filthier'n a sty by then, bacon grease an inch thick over everything, cigarettes all over, both me and LaVern'd smoked like furnaces back then...big pisspot full of diapers setting stinking next to the oil stove. I laid my ass out on the bed with this little pooch LaVern'd been give' by the people at White's tucked up next to me—Ginger we called her, smart little cocker-and-something-else bitch who used to sleep at my feet. So I laid back with more Gilbey's gin than I could put away in three days and I proceeded to get myself so goddamn polluted I couldn't hardly move...

"Next morning first thing I saw was this here hand, hide all ripped off the knuckles, thumb stove up...kind of thing I was used to, you know, waking up with your face sticking to the pillow, been in some brawl in some goddamn beer garden somewhere, hell, 'bout all anybody had to do in them days was look cross-eyed at me and I'd have a run at kicking the shit out of them.

"But I couldn't remember having gone anywheres. In fact I couldn't remember much of anything. I got up shaking like a rheumatic dog in trying to shit a peach pit...and there, laying on the pillow next to the one I'd slept on, was one of my guns, only

32

one I still got, a nine millimetre Steyr, don't have a clip, just a magazine in the handle and you stuff the shells in from the top. It had been full with eight rounds, but she was empty now, with the slide blown back...so somewheres or other the night before I'd emptied the fucker, and I thought Oh, no, I've up and done it this time, I killed somebody for sure...

"I rolled out of the sack and found me a stale beer. That moistened me up enough to try a little gin in a glass I'd left by the bed. Then I'd figured to go out to the outhouse and then come back and have me a real eye-opener of gin. I went into the kitchen on the way to the outhouse...

"She was a picture out of hell: blood, mine, from my hands, all over the place, the stove, the walls, the icebox, the kitchen table...there was cabbage-sized holes in the wall board where I must of staggered around some time or other the night before, blind drunk, beating the shit out of ever'thing. *Ever'fuckin'thing!* There wasn't hardly nothing I hadn't dented or busted or otherwise fucked up with these fists...

"And there by the outside door was Ginger where she'd been clawing at the bottom to get out. She was deader'n a smelt. Them eight rounds like to blowed her hind quarters off, like a rabbit hit about ten feet away with a twelve gauge. And the little dog, with her guts coming out her side, slippin' on 'em and not getting no traction, and pulling more of 'em out, wellsir, she'd dragged what was left of herself over to the door and clawed at it and died.

"There was this one moment while I took it all in, and then I wished to Christ I *had* gone out and killed some bastard in a gin mill...that would've been all she wrote and I'd of been marched off to Jackson Prison where I belonged...and at that moment I would of been happy to go...

"That one little moment took a lot of the starch out of me. It's the bottom of something when you get so drunk you got to take your meanness out on somebody, and then you find out that all you really done was to lay about your own household, knocking it apart worse'n your worst enemy would of done, and to top it off you ain't even brought down no enemy, no person you could look at and say, Well, if he's in there brawling and boozing like you, he's taking his chances, same as you...but no, all you done was to damn near bring your own house down around your ears as well as to murder this little creature that was the only thing around in them days could like you, no questions asked...

"Like I say, somehow that was all she wrote for my boozing...but it took a while. Quitting the sauce didn't kill *it*, whatever the sonofabitching thing inside me was that made me want to kill some other sonofabitch in a gin mill in the first place, in some ways that got worse for a while, until what I seen and was in in the South Pacific...that give me something different to think on...

"Anyhow, I did get myself up on the wagon, and in going on seventeen years I have not had even a single drop of beer. And I'll tell you, Miller, there's been a million times I wanted a drink—a million, you hear? But I have never once regretted quitting, never for one goddamn second. But you got to work on it—you cut out sauce and suddenly ever'thing's different than it was. You'd put up with shit like having to work and hangovers and all the rest, but just so's you could get back to your drinking, back to this little corner where nobody could reach you, and you'd try to keep yourself with half a bun on all the time you wasn't loaded, and your biggest fear, next to the shakes and the heebie-jeebies, was that you'd run out. When you quit, to make her work, you got to figure you'll never drink again—never. Hell, you can stop for a month or a year or twenty years and it ain't quitting: you got to do her for good. And when you do that everything's different.

"Anyhow, by the time I come back from winning the war against the Japs, LaVern'd divorced me and here you and Rex was, growing like weeds, still with Sonney and Pearl. I loved those people, still do, but growing up with old folks wasn't the thing for two young boys unless...well, I'd hit on a couple of notions in the South Pacific. First thing was to see what you boys thought of me. I was afraid Rex might recall what a son of a bitch I'd been, but he'd always seemed a forgiving sort and I figured you was probably too young to remember much. Maybe I really needed you boys more'n you needed me because without the war and without the sauce, I didn't know if I could fill in the hole them things left behind.

"Anyhow, I got set on getting me a chunk of land and not hardly moving off of her until I went out feet first...any goddamn thing'd do long's it was mine and I wasn't cheek-by-jowl with every son of a bitch in the county. At first when I come back I

34

didn't care how tough it was going to be, I was ready to start out in a pup tent and then cobble a shack together out of car bodies and tar paper to get me started if need be, hell, I figured I could live on squirrel and tree bark if I had to...

"But as it turned out I got this place and the house and buildings wasn't much, but I craved her almost with a hard-on ...maybe it was a mix of all that early boozing and then LaVern and then the war and...I just wanted this here one spot where I couldn't be got at for a while: I mean it was like I come home from three different wars, and I had me some energy going, but at the same time I was tuckered out from being around people, everybody, sergeants, lieutenants, Jap prisoners, whores, pimps, bastards, low-life scum of the earth...I needed me some peace and I knew I'd need it for the rest of my life.

"By then I'd decided I wasn't going to ever push you and Rex into nothing, insofar as it was possible. I wanted you'n him to make every fucking decision you could about your own lives. I figured trying to raise a kid right was about the biggest responsibility in the world, and there wasn't hardly nobody in the world truly up to it, let alone a reformed lush like your old man. And I knew your instincts was sound. So I figured I'd give you both the home and the patience and the loyalty as best I could and hope for the best...

"I'll tell you one thing, pal, so far I sure as hell ain't been disappointed."

*

When Miller rose unsteadily, so did Turner, moving to his side as though to assist him if he needed it. They stood together, shoulder to shoulder, and for long moments regarded through the living room windows the expanse of snow-covered cornfield to the right of the junkyard. Chill light from the bright splinter of half-moon spilled copiously over the rolling plain, now like a white lake, sparkling where the moonlight struck it as though all the waves of snow had been shot with minute bits of mica.

Butch, their year-old German shepherd, sighed blubberingly, thrashing once on his rug by the oil heater and then loosing an unconscious rippling groan of pleasure as wind roared in the flue.

35

"Don't drink any more of that damn coffee," Turner advised, "that was just for old Pop. Pulling a couple of drunk kids out of a car and bringing them home is big excitement for the old fart. But you're lucky it was him, though, 'stead of the state cops or sheriff or somebody. You know, back when I was boozing some son of a bitch was always trying to ram some hot coffee down me—don't know how many times I half-scalded my mouth and throat. Tell you what, Miller: go get the gin from the china cabinet, pour about a shot into a glass, fill it up with orange juice, and drink her down. Then go upstairs and hit the hay. You been a long ways today. I'll milk the cow in the morning and later on we can see to Rex's car. G'night, son."

Turner moved behind him. Miller continued to look out across the whitened field and at a glittering golden line of moonlight on the field's surface, pointing at him like a crooked finger.

Ice Fishing

I.

Miller Springstead dreamt: we are on Silverfish Lake, going ice fishing, me and Rex and Turner, I must be seventeen because it is Christmas vacation of 1957...

Details began to fill paucities: they had gotten their stuff together, kindling wood, can of kerosene, big scuttle of cannel coal, minnow bucket, tackle box, short ice fishing rods, half a fifty pound sack of crushed oyster shells, a spud, a sieve for an ice skimmer, the stainless steel thermos he and Rex had gotten Turner for Christmas full of coffee, a couple of Spam and cheese and mustard sandwiches apiece (I made them), and had stood there on the shore, looking out toward their shanty, a dot barely distinguishable from other dots in what seemed a vast whiteness.

As they'd stood by the public access's perimeter getting their stuff onto a sled Turner'd made from barn wood and truck springs, they'd heard a rustling a bit like cellophane being crushed as the branches in their thin shells of ice swayed and kissed and rubbed together in the faint cold breeze.

The Springsteads were heading out to their shanty a mile and a half out in the dead center of the lake, a tiny one-room cottage about eight by ten inside, with a little padlocked door and a stovepipe with a pointy cap like the kind in the *Smokey Stover* comic strip.

Miller and Rex fell a bit behind while Turner kept going at a good clip, tugging the sled, mackinaw collar up, ear flaps of his red cap turned down. Soon he was so far ahead they couldn't hear the crunch of his pacs breaking the snow's glassy crust. Each time Miller blinked his eyes, Turner seemed to jump ahead into the white distance.

In minutes Turner was already over halfway to the shanty,

37

tugging the sled, walking sturdily toward the barn-red shanty
with the white lettering above the door:

T. SPRINGSTEAD & SONS
ERMINE FALLS

Miller could barely see the other side of the lake three miles
distant where the summer homes of the Travises and Noels and
Braddocks and Dugalds were; the world was entirely composed
of dark blue sky and ice-covered snow with occasional flecks that
could be men or shanties, and on Turner marched, a diminishing
dark speck against the white.

*

Miller Springstead managed a bitter laugh, awakening,
some perverse part of him pleased that at this extreme stage he
could perceive and acknowledge dreadful irony—not for nothing
was he 25 and with two college degrees in English.

It was not 1957 he was awakening into, but bitter February
of 1966. And he was not awakening from some nightmare to find
himself home in bed, able to twist in the pilling flannel sheets
and tug tight the wool blankets over them, dimly aware of his
brother and father asleep elsewhere in the comfortable old
house: this time he was awakening from ice fishing into a
nightmare of now, on a metal bunk in a cell in the Skeegemog
County Governmental Center, hung-over, with no blanket nor
even a pillow and his brother dead.

So here in the now-quiet Skeegemog jail about an hour
before dawn he began to go over things, queerly quiet and even
studious in his contemplation, in contrast to all his shrieking
and hollering and reefing on the bars last night: *Motherfuckers!*
hadn't he screamed? *Sons of whores! Bastards! Lemme, out, I'll
kill him killed my brother—*

*

By noon day before yesterday I was already a little boozed;
I'd been sitting around in my apartment in Mt. Haven getting
ready to leave CMU for the last time. I'd finished my M.A. and
I was going back over my academic career, generously congratu-
lating myself: Well, Miller ole hoss, you may be from the boon-

38

docks but you sure can sling that academic crap about epiphanies and genres and gyres and objective correlatives and dissociations of sensibility, be it on paper or in person: why I do believe, if you don't hit a stump, you smart feller you, you may be a real mover and shaker yet. And all the while I kept pulling at that fifth of Jim Beam I'd got two months before but hadn't touched for fear I'd screw up my schoolwork, and I wanted my transcript just as she'll read, all A's and that one B+ in that goddamn criticism course.

My belongings were stacked up in cardboard boxes by the door, and it was getting dim out like it was going to snow hard: time to hit the road.

But I lingered, sitting there cross-legged on the bare floor, and in spite of my boozy self-congratulation the question came out of nowhere, like when you turn a flashlight into a blizzard at night and see the fusillade of flakes coming at you: *What do I want? What do I want?*

So naturally I had another drink and watched the seedy dump I'd lived in the past two years transform itself under the glow of the sauce until the familiar sagging floor and egg-yolk walls and curtains the shade of house mice seemed almost friendly.

What do I want? What the hell, who knew, who cared?

Action was the thing.

I bounced up and started running up and down the stairs like a coolie, bearing my boxes of books and junk down to my car, crazy to be on the road, to go home in what was after all a kind of triumph, to drive that hundred and twenty miles to the north as fast as possible in my creaking VW, to be back in my own country and able to present myself to my brother and father after having done well.

A light snow was just starting when I pulled out.

II.

When I get north, I find a note Turner's left tacked to the front door—"To Traverse, back for supper, Rex works to 4 to the Place—T"

Without going in, I head for Ermine Hills.

39

The VW ticks faithfully along Highway 31, and three miles south of our place, I turn into Ermine Falls proper. The old yellow brick school Rex and I attended has long since been torn down and town kids bussed elsewhere, and the town itself seems less a town now than a place where small roads from the hills converge and larger roads then diverge for other towns and distant freeway accesses.

Nothing moves in town except the lightly falling snow.

*

I park where paying customers—"guests"—park, not the area out behind the main kitchen the "help" is relegated to. Before me looms "The Lodge," an immense A-frame building behind whose deceptively rustic facade are mezzanines, curving staircases, endless expanses of glass, and carpeting so thick it feels bottomless; there are various banquet rooms on upper and lower levels with names like "Apple Room," "Smuggler's Cove," and "Serendipity," catering to whatever the moneyed pricks who command them want: convention parties, bachelor parties, receptions, who knows. From a variety of vantage points you can gaze at skiers descending the ski- corrugated and -latticed brow of Old Snowface, the most used and accessible of the Hills' several slopes. Naturally there are several bars in the Lodge.

*

In the main cocktail lounge murmurous sounds from the ubiquitous Muzak are light and festive. There are two customers at the bar, which is lined with Naugahyde and illuminated by tricky hidden lighting. A bartender is crouched behind it, holding a metal cannister against a savagely keening blender.

At various low tables about the room, ensconced on modernistic chrome and leatherette sling furniture, are a dozen or so skiers, returned from the day, smoking, drinking, still in ski garb, filling the air with strident hoots (Now that's what I call a *real* stem Christie!"..."Head over heels like you wouldn't b*elieve!* There was snow packed up my goddamn *nose!*") as they peer through the massive windows at skiers still whizzing down the darkening Old Snowface.

40

I sit at the end of the bar, the farthest point in the room from everyone else.

"Yes sir. What can I do you for?" asks the bartender, a ruddy, pleasant-looking man in his 50's whose belly has begun to descend toward his groin. His shiny ruddy head has a rime of white about the ears and side like salt on a Margarita. He wears a red satin vest and a black string tie.

"Ummm...I guess a double Jack Daniels Black Label on the rocks."

"Yes sir. Coming right at you."

I fork a ten onto the bar as he brings the drink and centers it carefully on a napkin. He doesn't take the money but puts the ticket he'd rung up on the chrome cash register behind him. He checks around for any signs of thirst, then speaks convivially to me: "Well, they say Snowface is getting worn down now so it's getting too fast for amateurs. Unless this little snow tonight mounts up, I suppose we'll have a rash of injuries again—how about those back slopes, eh, Thunderhead and Diamondback, I'll bet you that right now they give even Stein and Ian and Lars a run for their money—"

"Two daquiris, a dry Martini straight up, and a Brandy Alexander made with Grand Marnier!" cries a buxom girl in a white waitress uniform, evidently servicing a party in some other reach of the Lodge as well as helping out in the main bar. Hefty and robust, straw-blonde, vitality burns in the centers of her plump cheeks. Her hair is pulled into a loose ponytail, and she sticks out her full lower lip and blows up into some loose blonde tendrils over her forehead. She drums her fingers impatiently on the bar, muscles dance in her freckled forearm.

I am beginning to feel loose, comfortable, almost at ease. Hell, maybe after all, in spite of my contempt for the resort trash, it'd be a pleasant thing to have more money'n you could shake a stick at and be able to loll around night after night in a place like this, fawned upon by the management's sycophants as you drank yourself into a state of subtle euphoria.

"Hit you again?"

Before I can answer, the lights dim and "Dear Hearts and Gentle People" pulses from various speakers, and something turns hard in me—maybe it is the maudlin music, whose cloying lyrics I am compelled to recall: *I love those dear hearts and gentle*

41

people, who live and love in my home town...

Obviously this dipshit of a bartender has me confused.

There's a dream house, I'll build there someday, with picket fence and ramblin' rose...

Obviously he'd thought, upon seeing me in my parka and blue jeans, that I am somehow attached to those shitheads who know about slopes with cute names and Heads versus Fischers and who gossip knowingly about Lars and Stein and Ian and the other gigolo-athletes the management imports to wow the matrons.

So why not let him have it with both barrels: "Wal, yep, what the hell, why not, can't dance and it's too wet to plow, you might's well hotsy me on up 'nother one of them belts of old Brother Jack Daniels, and say"—one of his eyes is larger than the other, liquid and dark as old crankcase oil, and seems to distend at my words—"whyn't you just slap the mother on up here and say— my brother Rex Springstead, he works to the kitchen, I'd best get aholt of him, where's he at?"

The bartender blinks rapidly, steps coldly back several paces before calling out: "Fay! Hey, Fay!"

And there comes the blonde waitress, rushing in with a tray full of empty beer bottles. What lovely enormous tits.

"Fay, this guy wants to see Rex. See if you can get him, will you?"

"Sure." She tosses me a glance of curiosity, then speeds off noiselessly on sturdy nurse's shoes.

I am still waiting for the bartender, who has suddenly become absorbed in thumbing through a stack of receipts, to get my drink, and as I ready a command, Rex appears through the swinging doors at the far end of the bar. A wide grin splits his dark handsome face and his teeth are white as polished quartz; he is neat and clean in his checkered trousers and cook's tunic, except for dinner plates of dampness under his arms.

He is upon me in a second, and tears moisten the corners of my eyes. We clasp hands violently.

"Well, old Miller, how you doin', boy? I didn't figure you'd be along until tomorrow, I wasn't..."

"Hey, Rex, old buddy, Jesus H. Christ, you look fit as a fiddle'n prosperous as hell."

"Well, things are okay, got me that raise and I'm up to first cook now...how-do, Frank." He nods politely to the snotty bartender.

Beneath a patch with Rex's name in flowing red script is *Sous-Chef.*

"I work pretty hard at'er, Miller. Ra-ool, he's chef here, he's teaching me all kinds of stuff, plus I'm getting in some good overtime."

"Well, that's great...just like old whatsisass, Escoffier, huh..."

I am also keeping an eye on Frank, and fight to keep my hillbilly grin imposed over reluctant cheekbones: "Frank," I say pleasantly but distinctly, "Come here."

Rex is about to say something, but before he can a hand is clamped on his shoulder, and we both turn to see Ermine Hills' beaming owner, Milton Shelf. His hand lingers proprietarily on Rex. Shelf is small and thin, but wondrously erect, and he wears a youthful black and yellow striped blazer. Baroquely curliqued and graying hair on his wrists and hands gleams and his full slightly shaggy head of nearly white hair is given a gold sheen by the small recessed lights above him.

"So this is our college boy," Shelf says pleasantly, looking at me, his hand still on Rex's shoulder. "Say, Frank, fix the boys up with whatever their pleasure is. You're Miller, right? Well, I'm Milton Shelf, and I run this establishment." His hand is damp and firm; he gives me a brisk shake and drops my hand.

"Pleased to meet you," I say stiffly.

"Well, it's certainly a pleasure to finally meet you, too, Miller. Rex here, as you no doubt know, has certainly become a valuable asset to our little enterprise. Raoul, our chef, he's continental, has come to regard Rex as he does his own right arm. Well, now, take care, both of you—ah, there, I see Frank's set you up with what you were drinking before, Miller..."

I look around to confirm it; and by the time I look back, Shelf has stooped close to Rex so he can whisper briefly in his ear. Then he is off, his step light and springy for a man in his early 60's.

I turn to the new double and gulp it down; the fine whiskey burns like acid in my craw. "What was all that about?"

I am almost sorry Shelf left—I'd felt an impulse to slap the bastard with a couple of baroque sentences riddled with sonorous clauses clumped together like grapeshot just to show him I know where the bear shit in the buckwheat.

43

"Oh, nothing much, just for us to make sure this was our only drink here in the lounge..." Rex has a Blatz in front of him on the bar.

"The prick said *that*?"

"Well," Rex says defensively, "it's just Shelf don't allow the help to sit around boozing in any of the bars here. It's a rule. But you can have one drink. Hell, even Ra-ool don't take more than one, and he can do anything—but he just stops in for a Vermouth-Cassis every now and then is all..."

"Rex, I...what I mean is, what about *me*—*I* ain't the help around here, I'm free, white and over twenty-one and a citizen of the goddamned republic...shit, if I'd just wandered in off the slopes all done up like for an Abercrombie and Fitch ad and collared you and wanted to buy you a couple of drinks, you think I wouldn't be as welcome here as a goddamn inheritance?"

"Aw, c'mon, Miller," Rex says unhappily—"hey, you see the old man yet?"

"No. Hey, there, Fred, uh, no, *Frank*, right? Get me 'nother one of them double Jack Daniels, Frank, and snap it up—we got things to do and places to go and people to see."

Frank hesitates and looks questioningly over at Rex. "You know the boss only permits one drink at the bar for the help."

"Well, god-damn son of a bitch." I say it loudly enough to cause a woman at a nearby table to look over at us in startlement. "*I* don't goddamn work here. Shelf doesn't goddamn own me: I'm a *patron*. Frank, get me that drink."

"I'd advise you to keep a civil tongue in your head, young man," Frank says, dark liquid eyes narrowing, and all of a sudden I think I may have to reach forward and jerk this snotty son of a bitch across the bar by his Wyatt Earp tie, then fling him back against the bar mirror: I see him sliding to the floor, pulling with him, spectacularly, bottles of Courvoisier, gin, pernod, Jack Daniels. But I will accomodate Rex this time and not fuck things up for him.

"Well, don't sweat it, dipshit, to bloody hell with you—I believe my esteemed brother and I will go seek out some establishment around here that doesn't peer down its snotty nose at the, ah, indigenous citizens. Maybe there's still some place around that hasn't been ruined by Yahoos setting up plush tombs for the lolly-gagging of decadent scum—"

Rex crowds in close to me, shouldering between Frank and me, shoving me gently back, speaking cajolingly to Frank: "Hell, Frank, don't you pay too much mind to old Miller, he just get a wild hair every now and then, ain't that right, Miller?"

"That there's the truth just rat as rain, Clem, hee-yuck, hee-yuck, they ain't none of that makes me no nevermind, nossir!"

I boost myself off the comfortable stool to find myself almost staggering and actually in need of Rex to somewhat support me, turn me around, guide me—

We pass through swinging doors, Rex guiding me, then through another set of swinging doors marked KITCHEN, and past a figure to the right I only dimly glimpse, all in white, doubtless the legendary Raoul—so this is my introduction to him, shunted past his eminence, an oafish clown, gawked at by waitresses and busboys and potwashers.

"C'mon, take her easy, Miller," Rex whispers helpfully, "we'll just go on out the back way through the help's entrance..."

Far behind me I think I hear "Deep Purple" on the Muzak.

III.

I am in Rex's 46 Ford coupe, my vent directing a stream of chill air at my face, burning with shame: I wonder how much damage I've done my brother at the Hills. But when I look shyly at him, he is grinning widely, apparently not at all worried about any outrages committed by his hot-shot genius collegiate drunken asshole brother—

"Hey, Miller-boy, you sure as shit ain't crapping out on me *now*?"

I began a faltering apology: "Hey, listen, Rex, I really am goddamn sorry, the juice got to me, know what I mean, I didn't have any call to go shooting my mouth off to old whatsissass like that..."

Whop! Rex fetches me a solid jocular backhand blow to my breastbone: "Jee-*sus*, Miller! You see the look on that old prick's face? That son of a bitch thinks he's too good for the rest of us 'cause he's some kind of asshole buddy to the Noels, who're friends of Shelf, he thinks his shit don't stink, but he's finicky as an old woman...c'mon, gimme some of that Beam, I'm drier'n a popcorn fart..."

45

True, I seem to have the bottle; then I dimly remember getting it while Rex loaded some of my boxes from the VW into the trunk of the Ford.

The bottle is jammed tightly between my legs, so I uncap it and hand it over.

"Man, that fucking Frank, he hauled back like a poked snake when you give it to him like a professor, he didn't know whether to go shit or go blind...the busboys all hate his ass..."

*

We are cruising easily downhill through swirling flurries of light dry flakes. The hills and hummocks of snow on either side are luminescent beneath the strongly emerging half-moon, and for long moments I bathe my damp hands in the flow of hot air from the heater. As Rex is telling me about how we'd come pick up the VW tomorrow, I either fall asleep or pass out.

*

"What's up?" I ask, awakening, feeling half-way alert.

The car has stopped. "We home already?"

"Oh, just thought we'd stop in'n pick up a quick sixpack since we about done her to your Beam and I had 'bout all that shit I can handle...I ain't really much used to the hard stuff any more. Here, I'll tuck her up under my seat."

I discover we are at the Skeeg-Ho, parked between an old half-ton Ford pickup and a Hudson Hornet spotted like a leopard where patches of red primer reveals someone's work in progress. The only other car is a battered 51 Chevy.

Whirling snow has accumulated enough to crunch under our feet as we pass beneath the bar's sign, a huge predatory bird's head in profile, with a yellow eye and a savagely hooked beak. A handwritten note is scotch-taped to the vestibule door: UNDER NEW MANAGMENT.

The vestibule is close and dark and when I turn to see if Rex is coming he is dogging my steps so closely he runs into me, and we more or less fall into the bar proper like something out of the Three Stooges, giggling and hooting.

Rex shoves me on ahead of him toward the bar.

I belly up, then Rex lurches up against me and flings an arm around my neck for momentary support. His face is a bit pale and a loose grin quivers on his lips: "*Uh*-ooooohh...hey, Miller, keep tastin' a kind of saltiness back of my throat, know what I mean, I might be about to lose her, never can tell, think I'd best head for...the old...latrine..."

I watch him totter off uncertainly toward the far end of the building where a plywood stag's head, its features burned into its face, reads BUCK'S.

The bartender leaves off his conversation with the three other customers at the other end of the bar and ambles toward me; he too is keeping an eye on Rex's progress.

Then he is before me, a pallid, thin, unhealthy-looking gink in his forties, prematurely aged, with narrow shoulders both drooping and knobby. He squints suspiciously at me through the smoke of a small thin cigar.

"Two Blatz."

His sallow skin looks fragile as parchment and the whites of his muddy eyes are tinged with yellow. He plucks the half-smoked cigar from his mouth and grinds it out slowly in the ash tray no more than a foot from my face.

"Hey, pal, two Blatz."

"That guy sick?"

"Sick?"

"Feller back in the crapper."

A surly answer wells like risen bile in the back of my head, but I quell it: "Naw, naw, he's okay, he's my brother, he's just a little juiced is all—he's first cook to Ermine Hills is why he's got them checkered pants on, he'll be back in two shakes..."

"He ain't sick, huh? That ski-lodge crap don't cut no shit with me. I'm gettin' sick and tired of fuckers comin' in here and using my place for a toilet and laughing about it—night before last they was a guy cool as you please, one of them ski-boy hotshots, went back there and smashed out the fucking mirror in the towel cabinet I'd just fixed...ripped the apron off, puked on the floor, the son of a bitch..."

"Well, take it easy, pal, there's no skiers here—that's my brother and he's first cook—or hey, look at her this way, he's *from* here, hell, we both are, we grew up 'bout eight miles or so from here, just like—"

47

"I don't give a good fiddler's fuck if he's Lyndon Johnson's pot-warmer, you get him on out of there or I'm a-calling the Sheriff's, I've a-took just about all the shit I'm going to..."

Something quickens and tightens in me; I don't feel very drunk any more, but prickly, surly.

At the other end of the bar one of the trio there detaches himself from his pals and moves toward the jukebox against the wall, not far from the pool table. He leans back before the juke, thumbs in the loops of his jeans. He is short, nearly bald, and broad, about my size. The other two are taller and look like amiably juiced swamp-rat housepainters, dressed almost alike in paint-spattered jeans, hooded sweatshirts and insulated rubber pacs.

"Well, okay, listen, tell you what, I'll go check on my brother and make sure he don't fuck up your palace none, Ace, now just set them beers on up."

I turn to get off the stool, but there comes Rex out of the BUCK'S, making his way back toward me.

I shift around on my stool and the bartender grudgingly sets up two Blatz, two glasses, and takes my dollar bill.

I take my bottle by its neck and drink off half.

Behind me, the jukebox crashes into life, drenching us in a jangle of guitars and dobros:

> It don't hurt any more
> All my teardrops are dry...

Rex settles down next to me, and I look over my shoulder to see the stocky little guy still fiddling with jukebox buttons; he keeps time to the music with his feet, his unbuckled arctics flapping like a movie buccaneer's boots.

Sometimes when he shuffles his feet the top fasteners catch and cling together and you half-expect him to topple over into the juke.

The bartender slaps my thirty cents change on the bar and I turn to Rex: "How you doin' there, palzie? A little Blatz'll steady you down..."

Rex's eyes are a bit glassy, but he tilts his bottle back and sucks gamely at it. "Urp. Jesus, I couldn't bring it on up back in the can—but at least I pissed like a racehorse, and that done me some good..."

48

Time to change the subject: "Now, Rex, you understand I ain't tryinna get *nosy* or anything...but after all back at the Hills I seen that nice, big, good-looking blonde girl with the big tits keepin' an eye on you—*aha!* see you know who I'm talking about. Listen, you don't have to *tell* me nothing, I can use my imagination, but whyn't you just *smile* if you're getting any..."

Rex's grin practically starts in his balls and rises up through the Beam: "Ah, shit, Miller, old Miller, you don't know the fucking half of it—"

"Hat hare's Wa-aa-ahb Hearce!" the man at the juke cries loud enough to make me turn from Rex and look back at him.

"Ah, your ass sucks buttermilk, Peanut, that ain't Webb Pierce," one of his pals calls to him.

"How 'bout it, Ted?" the other one says to the bartender. "Who's the singer? Why'n hell can't you read who the singers is offa them cards on the juke?"

> No more walkin' the floor
> With that burnin' inside...

"Beats the shit out of me. That's the way the guy before me done her."

The guy named Peanut, back on his stool, beats a rapid tattoo on the bar with his hands, and I notice him staring pugnaciously at me. He calls to me: *"Hey, whad-dahell, tinkyaslookinsover, sumpin?"*

> No use to deny—I wanted to die
> The moment you said,
> We're thu-roo-hoo...

I slowly turn my back on him. "'Bout ready to haul ass, Rex? Be good to see Turner, good Christ, I am gonna sack out for a fucking week..."

I think of the upper part of our house which Rex and I have all for ourselves: of the hand-braided rag rugs thrown about, of my weights and bench and exercise equipment, of Rex's huge old closet full of clothes and guns, faintly odorous of Hoppe's Nitro Solvent No. 9 and dried wool; I see myself getting out an old pair of long underwear bottoms and crawling between those pilling

49

flannel sheets we use fall and winter.

"Okay by me," Rex says a bit groggily. "Let's get some air...fucking can back there stinks like empty shotgun shells."

We rise together from our stools, turn wearily toward the vestibule, Rex in front, all our ebullience gone.

I turn to get one last glimpse of the little pissant named Peanut; and I look about one second too long when I notice a scar on his upper lip like half a wishbone glued to it.

"Hooowadoin', lookinsover, sumpin'?"

I have got tired of deferring tonight: "'Fraid I can't make out what you're trying to say." Then, to one of his pals: "What's he trying to say anyhow?"

I know damn well what the harelip'd tried to say: *What are you doing, looking us over or something?*

"You guys just keep movin' on," the bartender says.

Rex grins obligingly and disappears into the vestibule.

I follow him for one step, then stop and slowly turn.

"You *git* right now or I'm a-calling the Sheriff's."

I ignore him.

"C'mon, now, Peanut," says the hillbilly nearest me without looking toward me. "This guy don't want no trouble...Peanut gets excitable, he thinks people're saying things about him, but he don't want no trouble..."

The other hillbilly says nothing.

"God-damnit, I've a-ready told you twice to *git*," the bartender says, taking a phone from its cradle somewhere beneath the bar.

I call over to Peanut: "I'm just plain sorry, there, Shorty, whyn't you clean the mashed taters out of your chops so's I can understand you?"

Peanut's stool clatters to the floor, and the other two, in spite of their collective bulk, have a hard time restraining his writhing, truncated form.

"Himmergo, Immagoinakillum, sumbish!"

"Take'er easy, Peanut," says the one on Peanut's far side, speaking for the first time.

"I've a-ready called the Sheriff's! I've a-ready called the Sheriff's!" the bartender cries.

The hillbilly nearest me says, "Maybe you all just better get on out while the gettin's good, buddy."

50

Peanut continues to struggle in his pals' grip, his face nearly vermillion.

"I've a-ready called the Sheriff's!" the bartender shrills again.

I turn on him: "For Christ's sake, I heard you the first time, swamp-rat, now kindly shut the fuck up!" I give him the finger and step into the vestibule, eager to move forward and out into the night.

The bartender cries out behind me, "You pricks from the ski business think you're King Shit—*Well, you ain't!*"

*

The bolstering bite of wind and snow feels good, and I turn my face upward . . . in moments snow has whirled up under the neck of my parka and condensed chillingly on my back and chest. It swarms about my face like white gnats.

Rex has been about to come get me. "I'll go get her warmed up," he says, "just wanted to make sure you was okay."

He staggers a little as he moves to the Ford.

"Maybe I ought to drive," I call after him, "case that asshole actually did call the cops'r somebody . . . I'm more or less sobered up, god-damnit . . ."

"Nah, I'm okay."

"Well, then, guess I'll take me a leak."

As Rex fires his engine, gunning it at first and then bringing it down to a smooth bubbling idle, I move to the old Hudson Hornet and begin watering its rear deck, enjoying the slowing of my heart and breathing after the near-encounter in the Skeeg-Ho. I write my initials on the car trunk.

I become aware of just how tired I am, how much I yearn to crawl into that car with its purple dashlights and feel the heater on my feet: again a vision of our upstairs drifts like a banner through a headache I've just begun to notice.

I am close to finishing when a two-year-old Oldsmobile with a dark bottom and white top and red flashing light mounted on its right front fender turns off Highway 31 and sides across the loose glittering snow of the Skeeg-Ho's parking lot, its lights flashing and winking as for some grand emergency, the engine gunning and tires spinning on the packed then dusted snow, the

51

whole car sideslipping to rest, finally, in the space between the Hudson and Rex's Ford.

I am still stuffing my cock back in my pants when out from the Olds lurches some kind of weird trooper in tall boots and hunting britches and a quilted nylon jacket with a badge on it, and a fur trooper's cap, with a badge on it, too: I barely recognize him as my old schoolmate and Rex's, Bernard "Burner" Dunstable.

My tongue freezes in my mouth as he storms awkwardly toward me like something out of a documentary on the rise of fascism, trying to pull a big, nickel-plated revolver from a holster like he is about to run John Dillinger to earth. He is easily two heads taller'n me and looks meaner than catshit in the light cast down from the single spotlight rigged from the telephone pole in front of the bar.

"Up against the wall, your hands inna air!"

I hear a squawk of gibberish from the police radio in the Olds, then I am shoved up against the Skeeg-Ho, Dunstable kicking my feet wide and frisking me: in spite of my fright I am almost ready to laugh at this whole thing: I am so weary, half-drunk, giddy, Christ, sometimes it seems you can't turn around without setting some Christawful machine in motion—*how did the bastard get here this quick?*

—*Luck!* Luck must had had him cruising nearby, probably on his way home from the Hills, and the Skeegemog dispatcher must have got the bartender's call and have reached Burner pronto—

"Stay there don't you move a inch!"

...Rex rolls down his window, hangs his head out and calls, "She's getting warm as toast in here, Miller. Hey, Burner, that you, you simple shit, ain't it late for you to be out playing cowboy? Thought you was working to the parking lot at the Hills all night, old Shelf'll have your ass f'you ain't punched out right again—"

—*"Get outta that car and get your hands inna air!"*

"Aw, shoot, Burner, you silly son of a bitch, quit'chur fuckin' around now, or you'n me'll have to tangle assholes again, and you 'member—"

I can smell peppermint schnapps even after Dunstable's left me to lurch to the Ford and jerk the door open—

"Well, you dizzy bastard, Burner, you look like you need a drink ...'sides, you're too big to kick the stuffins out of anymore,

52

tell you what, lemme offer you a jolt of this here panther piss of Miller's..."

I feel sick as I see Rex disappear and reach under the seat, see that big nickeled revolver come up and guess Burner is going to clout Rex over the head as he fishes for my Jim Beam—

—but then there are two quick sounds, *whomp-whomp*, like a light-gauge shotgun fired pointblank into an animal's den, and the interior of the Ford pops with lights like flashbulbs and for the briefest second I see the hulking form of Dunstable in front of Rex's open door, see the snow swirling around his huge shoulders and fur cap and sticking to them like salt, then my legs are pumping beneath me and there is a sound in my ears like pigs screaming as they're being castrated—

Just before I reach him, Dunstable turns sluggishly to meet me and it is simple to loop a leg behind him and shove him backwards: he topples over into some banked-up snow like a big old punky tree, his schnapps still in my nostrils.

As I dive into the passenger's side I see Rex, his mouth open, his tongue stuck out like a kid's, trying to say something, my name, maybe, and then his arms and legs flail briefly like broken cables and I scream out his name and there is a sound like trains coming and before I can reach and touch Rex a cave of darkness opens somewhere and swallows me.

Next thing I know I am in the back seat of a Michigan State Police cruiser, dazed, being ministered to out of a first-aid kit by a solemn young trooper about my age: twisting my neck, looking out through the cruiser's rear window, through the gusting, swirling snow, I can see the Skeeg-Ho and the clump of gawkers the disaster has brought forth, stamping their feet on the snow as they watch Skeegemog Country Sheriff's Deputy Bernard Dunstable and a Michigan State trooper loading a form covered and strapped on a stretcher into the rear of the hearse from Stinson's Funeral Home in Skeegemog which is often sent out to the scene of accidents because the Skeegemog Sheriff's Department doesn't have an ambulance.

IV.

I didn't see Turner until about eight-thirty. By then my head hardly throbbed any more, and I had earlier discarded the gauze and tape the young trooper'd applied.

Clyde Sturgis, who I used to arm-wrestle in high school some years back is a Sheriff's Deputy for Skeegemog County, just like Burner Dunstable, except he's full-time, and he brought me out of my cell and took me to a gloomy gray-painted room where in silence I stood before a wire cage like in a locker room and signed for and received my belt and an envelope with my billfold, jackknife, loose change and a Petoskey stone I carry for luck. Then he took me into the empty courtroom, and there by the judge's vacant dais stood Turner, looking much as he had when I saw him a few weeks ago when I was home for Christmas vacation, solid and powerful, wearing his red cap with the earflaps up and tied neatly across the top: surely he was the rock upon which my faltering strength could make some demands: *my brother your son is dead:* the information sat, a sullen, shit-eating dog, on the peripheries of my mind: I could recognize it as fact, yet something kept saying, *Hey, wait a minute, c'mon guys, let's back this thing up and we'll do it over again—*

"You stay loose, now, Miller," Clyde advised me in a kindly fashion from behind, doubtless recalling me last night screaming and hauling on the bars like a crazed gorilla.

Well, I wouldn't cause anybody any trouble, I had other fish to fry: for now that I had seen Turner, I knew I had to keep every fiber in me straining toward revenge: that as long as the thought of revenge could be sustained in my head, heart and balls, buffed shiny as a drop of blood by my rage, I could make myself hear Rex say, *Goddamn it now, you fix Burner's ass good and proper, Miller, don't let the fucker off Scot-free—I was just offering him a drink, not going for my little Ruger .22 like them pricks'll claim . . . if he done it to you, Miller, I'd get the fucker . . .*

But in seconds I knew Rex would really say to me, with infinite sadness, *Shit, nothing you can do now that won't make things worse, pal, it's all she wrote for me, do whatever the hell Turner says, give him a hand now—*

The door to the left closed behind Clyde with a hiss and we moved in the opposite direction toward a red-lit EXIT sign. Turner spoke to me low, not offering to shake hands as I had somehow thought he would: "Miller, I think you're off the hook, at least for now, for plowing into Dunstable, and anyhow the

54

state cops seem to be onto how he was drinking and they're going to investigate, ain't no charges against you...you look okay except for that lump on your head—how do you feel, buddy? Okay?"

A babel of protesting voices from all my selves screamed in unison in my head, *Okay, okay, my ass, we gonna get that fucker Dunstable, make him the sorriest fucker this side of the Spanish Inquisition*—"Okay," I muttered hoarsely, "okay."

But in the pickup, before it warmed, while the smoky vapor of our breath pulsed in and out, I found the murder I sought in my voice: "I am gonna fix that sonofabitch Dunstable if it's the last goddamn—"

"—No!" Turner's broad raised hand was like a paddle.

His thick strong fingers trembled slightly, and I looked away, out the window at the threatening sky slowly turning black as death's crêpe.

I was silent for just a moment , then leaned forward: "What the hell you mean *No!*" I cried, "why, if it's the last goddamn thing ..." But I stopped when I saw Turner's eyes: they were not hurt or sad or angry, but empty.

Without another word, Turner put the pickup in gear and drove home.

*

The day remained leaden. We sat in the living room, silent, Turner in his easy chair arranged by the window so he could look out at the cornfield north of the junkyard, all of it covered now with snow. Turner didn't take off his hat and coat, but just sat there, silent, looking out at the expanse of snow-covered cornfield. Not once did his vision stray left to the tangled metal of the yard.

I slouched back on the sofa, and after a while, I pulled an old afghan Pearl knit years ago from the back of it, wrapped it around me, pushed my boots off and lay face down.

Sweet fatigue overtook me quickly and gently, mercifully. I burrowed forward into a cushion, and in moments we were all going ice fishing again.

We were in the shanty and Turner got the little stove going and put on some coal while the pine kindling still snapped. Then he used the spud to jab away the inch or so of ice that'd formed in the square hole in the shanty floor.

Rex skimmed the loose ice off with the sieve, I got our folding chairs situated, Turner poured us each a cup of coffee, and soon we had shucked down to our shirtsleeves and began to get ready for some fishing.

Turner threw handfuls of crushed oyster shell into the clear water of Silverfish Lake and we watched the flashing bits spin slowly down some forty feet, creating a glowing circle on the sandy bottom.

Then Turner stuck some Red Man in his jaw and pulled an ash-filled tomato can close for a cuspidor.

As the odors of chewing tobacco, coal, the steaming rubber bottoms of our pacs, rose around us, we looked to our sawed-off rods and stuff and baited the hooks with minnows, impaling them just under the dorsal fin; crouching forward on our creaking canvas chairs, we sent them into the water, their silvery sides flashing like bits of jewelry as they rotated downward.

Perch swam into view. We could see them clearly against the numinous glow created by the oyster shells. We tried to tempt them, sometimes successfully, sometimes not; we threw the little ones back, put the keepers on a stringer so they floated alive just under the shanty.

Sometime later when Turner cleared his throat and spat into the tomato can, I suddenly knew it was time to go home—but I didn't want to: I wanted to stay forever in that cozy little pocket of warm and dark and father and brother and ice fish on.

Turner brought his railroad watch close to his face, crouched close to the stove so he could read the dial by streaks of firelight showing through cracks in the stove.

"Jesus, where did the time go? We better get a wiggle on... and all we got's this itty-bitty string of five perch and one measly bluegill, hardly enough for a proper mess."

"We can hang around and get some more," I said hopefully.

"We could but we can't."

"Holy Jesus!" Rex cried suddenly, falling to his knees, arms planted on either side of the square hole, gawking into the water: "Lookit that son of a bitch!"

Turner and I leaned forward, craning our necks, but Rex was in the way. He moved aside then and through the darkening portal of clear water, near the bottom, lingered a huge black fish;

56

even considering the water's magnification he must have been at least five feet long, graceful as a torpedo, pectoral fins wavering slightly, not moving himself so much as drifting over the glowing bed of oyster shells.

"What in hell's that?" Rex cried. "What is it, Turner, that a Muskie?"

Turner drew closer, fascinated, squinting.

"It ain't some kind of freak Great Northern or a gar or some damn thing, is it? Ain't it too big in the...shoulder or something, Turner?"

"Hmmm...ain't a Muskellunge," Turner said thoughtfully, "you're right, too big towards the rear and Northerns don't get that big...guess he's an old mossbacked sturgeon, loafing along and taking her easy, feeding off the bottom..."

"Damnit," I muttered fretfully, "should of brought Rex's sucker spear and a Muskie lure, we could of lured the bugger up and then—"

"—No," Turner interrupted me gently. "No, you shouldn't, hell, give the old pal a break, Miller, don't be so goddamned bloodthirsty. Those old bastards, those bottom feeders, they don't even have teeth."

"That right?"

"Yeah, just hard lips, kind of...some of them live to ripe old ages, they get to be fifty or sixty. I reckon old Grandad there's come from Lake Michigan into Grand Traverse, then as a youngster probably got through the power plant at Elk Rapids into Skeegemog Lake, then into Silverfish. Have a heart—don't let it be you that spears him and mounts his head on the wall— leave that for the resorters...good luck, pal..."

The huge ghostly fish below, barely visibly as the light continued to fall, drifted slowly out of sight.

V.

It is nearly dark when I awaken, and no lights are on in the house. Turner still sits where he was when I drifted off, and he still hasn't taken off either mackinaw or hat. I twist around on the sofa, hugging the afghan to me.

"What're we going to do now, Pa?"

57

"Do?" His head swings, I see his eyes in the gloom, and I think of the buckets of cold ashes he used to shovel from the furnace before we started to heat with oil. "Do?" Something like a sneer twists his lips. "Good Christ A-mighty, here you are twenty-five years old and with two college degrees and you have to come to your old man who runs a junkyard in the boondocks and say to him, What are we going to do, Pa? Do about what?"

"Why about Dunstable," I say rapidly, "why, we got to do something about Rex..."

"Rex is dead," Turner says shortly, focusing those dead-ashes eyes on me. "And what the hell do you do when somebody's dead? Why, you mumble some words if you're of a mind and then you stick them in the ground like you'd do with tainted meat. There's no real difference between a corpse and a mound of shit. Don't you with all your brains understand it's the end of *doing* things?"

"It ain't the end of nothing!" I cry, "not while that murdering scum Burner Dunstable is free to walk the earth. I tell you, before I'm through with the son of a bitch—"

"You'll shit, too, if you eat green apples," Turner interrupts sourly. "Anyhow, you got the wrong man, Dunstable ain't a man but a thing—"

"—Wrong man, my ass!" I explode, "Turner, Jesus, I fucking *seen* Rex's arms and legs moving like a shot animal's, I *seen* the blood on his lips, I *heard* the goddamn gun—"

"No." Turner holds up his hand to stop me. "No."

"*No?*"

He sighs, looks out again at his cornfield. "Sometimes you ain't so smart," he says, but gently. "Listen. A fool kid burns down your house, who do you call to account? Him, the kid, for being a nut? His folks for bringing up a firebug? The match company for the wherewithal? The year? The country? The world? You tell me, buddy. What I'm trying to say is, the chickens have come home to roost closer'n you seem to be able to understand..."

"What in hell are you talking about?"

Turner jerks a thumb at his heart: "Here's where she is, pal," he says.

"*What?*"

"I done it. I killed Rex. Or I might as well of. Dunstable don't matter, he's got no more wit than a rabbit or a toad. You ain't got to look that far afield for your culprit, Miller, he's right here."

"*What?*"

"So I went ahead and tried to set up my own little world with me as a kindly old God and I figured that coupled with you boys's instincts would be enough to get us by...but what I should of known, pal, should of known, what I should of known all along was, I couldn't bail out of things like that just to ease my set of war nerves, and I guess I knew her in my bones long before this. Ah, Christ, maybe if I could of married again..."

"That ain't the way it works, Pa," I say, "you done your best and me and Rex got to own up to our fucking up, especially *me*, shit, I'm more to blame than anybody..."

My words cease, for Turner has been shaking his head, each movement negating whatever I might say.

"Let me tell you how it works," he says, voice down to a gravelly whisper with something liquid in it, a slight rasping of phlegm around the edges of his words. "You talk about your responsibility. You *seen*, you say. Goddamn right, but you just seen what the tab is; now I'm telling you where the buck stops: it's here." This time he jabs his thumb forcefully into his chest: "And here's why this is your culprit: because the more you understand all this, the *more* responsible you are. At the root of her all was me giving myself what I wanted and saying it was best for you guys. And that kind of selfishness hooks up real nice with some of the nasty pits and sharp edges the world can dish you up. You got the cloth to cut how you will, and not making the best of her is about as close as I can come to giving sin a name..."

His voice trails off into silence, his head begins to lower toward his cupping hands, and as I watch with horror, Turner falls into the abyss he has just created: I'd rather pitchfork maggoty corpses into wheelbarrows than watch, yet there's no not watching: it is falling backwards into a dim stairwell, drowning in a night of spilled ink.

Like the first fissure that appears in a sheet of ice unable to bear your weight as your boot descends ever more heavily upon it, so does Turner's face crack: the weathered skin still bright as a child's in the centers of his cheeks whitens and tightens inward, wrinkling around the eyes the way lips do around toothless gums, the mouth comes open as though he is choking on some fearsome bone, the eyes pinch all the way shut...one tear comes from one eye, one from the other, then my old man, Pa, Turner, Turner Springstead, is weeping, monstrous palsied shudders that sweep through his powerful frame like brushfire; waves of grief and despair course through him, the soul's dry heaves, the dreadful inevitable fall of the other shoe; and suddenly I know the most terrific thing a son can see is the defeat by life of his father; and it is even worse when the son has assisted in the destruction.

Turner shudders on and the first true knowledge of Rex's death falls across my shoulders like a shawl of lead.

I rise from the sofa, letting the afghan fall on the floor, and numb with my own culpability blindly seek the china cabinet where despite Turner's many years of tee-totalling a bottle of gin has always been kept for guests.

What The Moon Said

...there, rimmed by the fuzzy perimeters of Miller Springstead's dream, was the movie screen: a huge white rectangle painted on the bricks of the northern side of Guilder's General Store in Ermine Falls.

It was nearly seven-thirty and the outlines of the screen were feathering into the yellowing bricks. The corners of the screen were rounded like the corners of sepia-toned photographs in archaic photo albums.

It was Friday of the second week of September and of the first week of school, and fall was in the air—earlier, the sun had guttered out like dying embers, and a harvest moon fat as a pullet's breast was rising in the east.

It was 1958, and this was to be the last free show the town would ever have—the merchants who paid the itinerant projectionists who serviced Ermine Falls and other such towns had reached the point of diminishing returns in their sponsorship, or so the story went.

Miller wasn't inside Ernie's Sinclair, leaning across the pop cooler and looking across the road at the half-acre field in front of the screen where the stilted projectionist's booth was outlined against the white of the screen like a blade sight on a rifle.

Sure, there you were, outside, more or less out of sight, leaning up against the cool clapboards of the gas station, touching your hurt places, your puffed cheek and swollen nose and split lip as you watched your countrymen streaming into town in their old pickups and sagging Plymouths and Fords and Chevys. There were the Blackwells, all eight of them, in their rusted-out Henry J with shocks so bad it lurched up and down as it moved slowly along. High school kids, packed into their Fords and Mercs, were making their entrances and exits all around town. Some cars were shackled so low in the ass their bumpers'd scrape

61

gravel and throw sprays of sparks when they'd catfuck around a corner—later you could probably even find where somebody's fender skirt'd scooped out a trench like a spoon drug across butter.

Free show. Miller spat on the ground to his left. That brought them in all right, "to town," to squander their nickels and sweat-worn dimes and soft creased dollar bills on ice cream, potato chips, funny books, baseball caps, pork rinds, bottles of RC Cola down which nickel sacks of Planter's peanuts were funnelled, then extracted into the mouth with sips of pop.

And there I was at eighteen when the faintest suggestion of pussy is enough to make your short hairs stand on end and set your parts aquiver. And on that night I had a date with a cute little quiff from Les Champs du Roi, the summer resort on the northwest corner of Silverfish Lake. It was a time when I should have been jumping for joy: why here you are, Miller, just a swamp-rat, yet damned if you ain't got some small purchase on the affections of Sandy Dehner from Cincinatti; no more scratching after these thick-ankled duck-butted potato-fed dragnasties from around here...Sandy Dehner was coming for me in her father's red Thunderbird.

But reason I wasn't all bushy-tailed and feeling my oats was because between the two days ago when I'd met her and tonight I'd had that run-in at school and been suspended for three days and I looked like a Mack truck had run over me.

I heard the scratchy, erratic whisper of a needle on a barren record groove, then music bathed the crowd slowly encamping on the ground in front of the screen with blankets and bottles and things to eat:

> Love oh love oh careless love
> Oh you see what love has done to me

A kid named Harlan Flanders had transferred into Ermine Falls last week, and he'd started out noisy as hell, pissing and moaning on every occasion how fucking awful it was that his old man'd got sent from Saginaw to being a foreman of the cement block plant outside of Skeegemog. And naturally my pals, the local clucks, all applauded him for it, and listened with something bordering on awe as he spun his yarns of city life, thinking: Wow, right, we gotta get us some of whatever's he's got. Not to mention he seemed as exotic to the local pussy as a sable or ocelot coat— hell, getting him some nookie off the quiff of his choice would've been like potting fish in a barrel.

Too bad for him that before he ever got around to it he and I went at it with the result that his old man sent him off to military school in Connecticut.

Later, when I was at Central State in Mt. Haven, I came to realize that Flanders had somehow been the archetype for the suave, dapper, elegant frat-rat I was both fascinated and repelled by, the dreamboat decked out in his fastidiously pressed Gant shirts and trim chinos—who no matter how much I disparaged him had a kind of snotty grace that permitted him to loll around with his Sig Ep or Delt Sig or whatever- they- were buddies, a tan trenchcoat and an umbrella draped over his arm when there was no need of either.

Anyhow, in spite of what it cost him and me, I fixed old Flanders' ass. But now my face was swollen like a clown's and I feared—expected—Sandy Dehner would take one look at me and say, "Oh, you uncouth lout—ick!" And flee...

*

It hadn't begun as a match between himself as the local tow-headed strongboy versus the dapper urbanite from Saginaw who'd already fought in the Golden Gloves and who was tall and lean and handsome, with a remarkable grin that seemed to sneer and as well exhibit his beautiful teeth. It had started on Wednesday with Flanders coming up to Miller during the Free Gym period when the phys ed teacher and coach were gone ("Jee-sus, they call this a *gym?*") as Miller worked out in solitary concentration on the parallel bars ("Go in for that gymnastic stuff, huh—gotta watch out so your legs stay in shape..."). He had chattered on about boxing ("I mean if you had the right equipment here I bet I could show you guys a thing or two..."), and before Miller had grasped what was going on, Flanders was offering to give him a few pointers on boxing ("Show you what I mean about timing..."), Flanders getting his own gloves from his locker, leaving Miller to use the single pair Ermine Falls Community School owned, twelve-ounce ones with the laces permanently tied so you could slip your hands in and out with ease ("Want to show you how reach can help the taller man...").

How things so rapidly accelerated into the real fight that the next few minutes became Miller didn't understand; but he quickly found himself bloodied, rubber-legged, fighting not to win but to avoid stumbling drunkenly, and being humiliated before the classmates that had before because of his unquestioned strength thought him so formidable. Yet still he stood, not knowing what else to do, ready to take more of the thrashing the treacherous Flanders was joyfully administering with the widest grin imaginable—"What a glutton for punishment," Miller heard somebody say from the edge of the wrestling mat on which they boxed.

I reckon the one lesson I learned then as at no other time was the meaning of technique: for that rather than speed or strength was what gave Flanders the edge: Christ, he was slicker than snot, trying to get to him through his punishing lighter gloves was like dipping your hands after a fish. Somewhere in the back of my head I could hear Turner growl, *Well, maybe next time somebody says to look up his ass and see if there's a locomotive coming you'll think twice—*

Miller was ready to go until he dropped, but suddenly Flanders stopped and with a grin at once contemptuous and magnanimous said, "Lookit, Springstead, your goddamn nose's bleeding all over my gloves, these're good ones my old man got for me and I'm not gonna ruin'em." And for the half-dozen spectators he raised aloft his expensive gloves, clasping them together as he declared himself the winner.

Tottery and bruised, bleeding still from his nose, Miller walked trembling toward the showers.

Before a washbowl and mirror he began cupping paper towels sodden with cold water against his bleeding nose and ragged lips. Even one of his ears was bleeding. Then when the blood was stanched and he was examining himself in the mirror, he seemed to see his father's face beneath his own, the same salient cheekbones, same light blue eyes, and as he continued to stare, he thought he could see Turner's square jaw superimposed over his own more rounded one.

And as I continued to look into my own confused and hangdog eyes I could see some of his energy trying to fill them.

64

Something hot as sex grew within me and suddenly I recalled something Turner'd said once during one of those talks we'd sometimes have in the winter when I'd maybe come downstairs at three in the morning to take a leak and get a drink of water and there'd be Turner, listening to his Sky Buddy, drinking coffee and looking out across the cornfield covered with snow: *Sometimes when you got to do something you think you can't, well sometimes you can, but you got to bring every ounce of energy you have to bear on this here single problem, like there's just this one goddamn thing in the whole world to be done and you're the machine to do her—those ain't your arms and legs, they're cables and levers and they was made for one thing, to do this here one thing before you...*

I blinked and when I looked into my eyes they weren't mine: a clear light'd come on behind them: it was like watching a movie and living in it at the same time.

I went back out onto the gym floor where a few seniors were still flocked around Flanders like autograph hounds; Tommy Nuenshwander was untying the laces on Flanders' gloves for him, saying, "Man-oh-man, I never seen nothing like that, you really trimmed old 'Stead's feathers for him—"

"I'm back," I said, tapping Flanders on the shoulder with one of those spongy school gloves and smiling myself into his beautiful and confident smile.

Tommy and the others drew back as Flanders with a look of feigned weariness lifted his gloves. Just as they rose I launched myself at him, catapulting forward all whirling cogs and levers and cables and mallets and booms and away we went—

The funniest part was, there was no rage in me. I knew what I was doing, saw it more clearly than it seemed I'd ever seen anything in my life: Oh, I bulldozed into him with a flurry of sodden but tireless blows not minding where or if I was hit as my arms kept punching and hammering, until he slipped moving back away from me and I rode him down onto the mat, all the while bludgeoning him with the puffy gloves, finally using them like mallets on his nose and mouth as he futilely writhed beneath me, I beat on him until his mouth looked like mashed cherries. They were trying to pull me off him then, and so I let them seem to restrain me until Flanders got himself shakily up from the mat—then I broke loose and got to him one last time, gathered him to me in my arms for a moment and stepped off the mat and flung him like he was a feedsack against the folded-up bleachers. I reckon it was then he broke his collar bone.

I lowered my suddenly heavy arms and went back toward the showers.

*

Late that afternoon, well after the last bus had left, Miller sat rigidly in one of the uncomfortable chairs—purposely so, he suspected—in the office of the Superintendent, Barton Mildwood, whom all the kids called Woody behind his back. Mildwood was spare and gray and his prim mouth was as usual pursed in some obscure negation as he shuffled through a sheaf of papers on his desk. Both he and Miller were waiting.

Then the omnipresent buzz from the fluorescent lighting was snipped neatly as with clumps of his work shoes Turner Springstead entered the office, a black wool watchcap in both hands over his groin. Turner's presence seemed to reduce the office's space by half and Miller instantly felt a little better.

"Mister Springstead, come in," Mildwood said, although Turner was already in.

Miller's mind had been jumping around during the dreadful wait and now he thought back to Christmas Eve when he was sixteen: That big ginned-up Polack hayseed must of been six-three and he come into the shop pissing and moaning about how we'd sold him a bum four dollar water pump off a 47 Caddy that Turner let him take off himself to give him a break on the price, even lent him the goddamn tools.

That big dumb-looking shit slammed that goddamn pump down and greasy water leaked onto the counter where Turner was drinking coffee out of his thermos top and looking up something in one of the part books mounted there by the register.

Goddamnit! the Polack yells, This'un ain't no good and I want my money back—now!

Turner looks up slowly, eyes bright and alert as a chipmunk's, and says quiet-like, Hold her down, there, Ace, we don't holler like that in my shop.

Your shop my ass! the gink yells, you don't gimme back my four bucks right now I may rip the shit out of something!

66

Well, says Turner, still speaking low and reasonable, I sure hope you don't try—getting riled ain't good for my condition.

Yeah? You don't say—what's your condition? the guy says, starting to feel pretty good, like he's gonna be a winner without no problems.

I'm a pacifist of some kind or other, Turner says.

You don't say?

That's right, something I picked up in the Corps. See, if you was to hit me, I might not even hit you back.

That so?

But if I figured you was about something that might be a threat to my kids or my house or my dog, why then—

Turner's arm moves in a blur and there's an awful crack like a rifle shot and dust and grit fly from where he's sunk the hook end of a small crowbar from under the counter into an upright about two inches from the guy's head.

Polack jumps back, eyes fluttering from the grit in them, fists up, and Turner tugs on the crowbar that's sunk deep into the wood; it makes a rending sound—CRICK!—like rusty old gates being forced open.

By the time he's freed the crowbar and started to come around the counter, the Polack, who'd started backing up ever since the steel went into the wood, is out the door, his greasy water pump still lying on the counter.

"...and the report I got half an hour ago from Munson Hospital in Traverse City is that the Flanders boy has a broken collarbone, which I trust'll mend well since he's a young man. But more troublesome is the loss of his teeth, particularly the front ones...but please—sit down, Mister Springstead..."

All I want for Christmas is my two front teef! Miller sang giddily to himself. Tell'im how it is, Turner—

Turner eased himself down carefully into the spindly chair before Mildwood's desk, face blank and noncommittal even to Miller, hands still sunk into the wool of his watchcap...then Miller noticed something small beginning to twitch rhythmically high in Turner's cheek.

"...and, uh, just how seriously it's being taken can be gauged from the fact his father is already considering withdrawing him and sending him East...Mister Flanders in fact had hoped to meet with us but he's presently at the hospital..."

Turner's head moved slightly up and down in acknowledgement. And finally spoke: "Wellsir, I'm real sorry it all happened, Mister Mildwood, and I don't know quite what to say. I reckon if there's any medical expenses that insurance don't cover I'd be happy to make it up. I'm real sorry Miller here took it into his noodle to go for the other boy as rough as he did. Maybe neither Rex nor Miller gets as much as they need at home—it's near always been the three of us batching it out to the yard, and that maybe makes a boy harder in some ways and softer in others than your run-of-the-mill town boy. But I do believe it'd be a terrible mistake if you was to go ahead and suspend Miller for two weeks like you mentioned, and I'm hoping you won't do that..."

Miller realized suddenly that not once since his father had come into this office had he looked at him.

"...I'm 'specially worried what it'd do to his schoolwork, which he's real serious about. Like you know probably better than anybody, Miller's got a real good mind for school and I aim to see him get to college one way or the other..."

"Ah. Well, you're certainly correct as to his academic potential, but this is a pretty serious business and I'm getting some pressure from the Flanders boy's father as well as...well, let me ask you outright, then, Mister Springstead: Miller seems clearly at fault here: what do you think would constitute an appropriate punishment?" Mildwood leaned back in his swivel chair, lips pursed, and carefully interlocked all but his index fingers, which he slowly pressed against his lips.

"Well." Turner raised his thick fingers, shadowed by the all-but-impregnable grit from work, and massaged the shiny fore portion of his scalp while a thumb meditatively scratched an ear. "Hmmm. That's a tough one. But what if you was to do this: give him a three day suspension because you got to do something like that. And I'll promise to do the rest. I'll see he don't do nothing in a social way for, say, a month, and I'll see he's got enough work to home to keep some of the starch out of him. That and his homework ought to keep him out of mischief and occupied in a useful way. And I'll see if I can't make sure he don't get into no more things like this—though from the looks of things, the other boy seems to've got in some good licks too, and while I'm real sorry about the Flanders boy, I hear there's some dispute about

68

who started things up... though I grant you there ain't much about who finished them..."

Turner still hadn't looked directly at Miller.

Mildwood slouched back into his chair, then came thoughtfully forward and leaned his elbows on his glass-topped desk, his gray gaze skimming over his steepled fingers at Turner. And he nodded.

*

It was doubtful, Miller later realized, that he'd have assailed Turner as he did when they got home and were seated on the living room sofa, had Turner once looked at him when they were in Mildwood's office. That rankled most.

"But Pa...hell, Turner, you didn't have to practically kiss his ass to get me off the hook, Christ, lettim do what he wants with me, Christ, you treat him like you think he's a better man'n you are or something..."

Turner raised his right hand, held it up imperiously, to stifle his son. "He is," Turner said mildly.

Something cold and slimy turned over in Miller's stomach. *"What?"*

"Better'n me." Turner looked Miller fully in the face but his look was if anything bland, unreadable.

"What? Christ's sake, Pa, what're you talking about? Look what you done! And not just in the war and all! Christ, you're like old Ben Franklin in my tenth grade history book that you liked so much, coming to Philadelphia with two pennies and spending'em on bread and standing there munching them loaves, and then going to..."

Turner's hand started to lift from his knee to make his familiar paddle gesture, but he lowered it. "Look at it this way, Miller," he said mildly, "now you may think Mildwood's kind of a prick, and in a lot of ways he ain't my kind of guy, but he's had the wit and energy to get himself in the world where he does something important, hell what could be more important than teaching kids...and goddamnit, he's earned his respect. So yeah, I'm happy to admit he's a better man'n me. But don't get me wrong: there's times I'm so happy to just be a junkyard guy tucked off in the Michigan boondocks I don't know whether to go

69

shit or go blind. Miller, you got no idea what a mine is like, or even a Ford plant, they're a kind of living death. But you, goddamnit, you got ever'thing in the way of wherewithal that counts, a quick mind and a knack for schoolwork...maybe ever'thing you need except not having a ma as you grew up, which may've hurt some corner of you, but never mind, we ain't able to do nothing about that at this stage in the game. But if you don't get you a giant thirst like the one I had that damn near did me in, then there ain't no limit to what you can do, *no limit atall, you hear—*"

*

"No fucking limit, I hear you," Miller Springstead muttered aloud in Iowa City in August of 1967. He snorted, twisting on the bed, trapped like a fly in amber in the demi-monde between sleep and waking. Then at last some part of him left the submerged, shifting currents of memory, rising like a trout toward the nightbug of consciousness. His eyes opened. Turner had stuck out his hand: "Are we agreed, son? Then put'er there."

Agreed upon what, exactly? But no matter, I took that big warm strong hand, God I took it...

It was dark and he lay naked on the bed, curled into himself like a grub as for warmth, though the humid summer night had already caused him to soak the sheets through.

He turned his head to the left; Lindsay hadn't taken the alarm clock when she'd gone back to northern Michigan yesterday to "sort things out," so the luminous wheel was where he'd expected it to be, and at the hour he'd also somehow expected it to be: three in the morning.

He got up and lurched to the open window and thrust the curtains apart. A full moon rode high in the east, and as the dew on the Springstead's minute back lawn refracted its light, the grass began to glitter. He flexed his right arm, feeling with the fingers of his left the hard ball of his biceps, loving and hating it at the same time, this rugged and durable peasant's body, designed, so it seemed, if not to rend and tear and break, then at the very least to tote and pack and hustle...coolie work.

In Elizabethan times I bet I'd've made a great headsman.

Sometimes I reckon this body's defined for me what I'm to be, am, telling me the way October sings in the blood that I was never cut out for a sleek and gorgeous article like Lindsay, no, I was made for country pussy, good-natured humble-bunnies whose point in life comes on Friday and Saturday nights in the taverns and a lot of abandoned and sodden screwing afterwards ...the kind of girl who starts to have kids and thicken in belly and hip, then to take on a certain slackness of haunch and ham as she creeps toward unkemptness and frowsiness. And with such a woman I suppose instead of being the binge-drinker I am I'd be the real thing, the chronic alky, the guy who discovers that a whole lot of this crap called life ain't so bad if you can just keep a couple of belts in you all the time for general looseness.

I reckon if the thing with Flanders didn't do it, the thing with Sandy Dehner did: made me admit there was others in the world intrinsically better than the Springsteads, better in the blood and the marrow and the bowels and the luck—it seemed like you had to learn, first off, that others could have something you never could, and if you did seem to be on the right track sometimes, it was just like somebody feeble-minded showing mastery of a Jew's Harp. In short, there seemed to be a fineness in grain that others had and that you could never attain.

He massaged his flexed arm and thought ruefully, Not too bad for a guy heading for his late twenties, almost as good as when you were a teenager.

The moon seemed to burn like summer sun across his face, and he shivered. From somewhere out beyond his yard he thought he could hear the ghostly strains of music: *Love oh love oh careless love...*

Miller knelt by the bed and found a nearly full can of Budweiser; it was warm, but fizzed when he brought it trembling to his ear. He drank, gulping it down like an antidote, and was rewarded: a slight glow, pleasant easement, bitter satisfaction: no matter how fucked up you were, there was this. As the poet said, Sleep is too short a death.

Another few swallows and he'd drained the can. No matter, there were plenty more in the refrigerator, he remembered, plus a fair supply of Jim Beam.

"Free show, my ass," he muttered on his way to the kitchen.

With another beer and a shot of Beam warming him, Miller lay back on the bed, staring at the dim rectangle of the ceiling, palely luminous from moonlight spilling through curtains he'd recently parted.

So he was eighteen and waiting for her while the moon got higher and higher and brighter and harder-looking.

> My heart cries for you
> Lies for you
> Dies for you

whined across the tipsy, giddy crowd sprawled before Guilder's, waiting for the show to start. Krazy Kat was over and now there was a long intermission as they changed the reels to Laurel and Hardy and thus encouraged people to buy still more things to eat and drink before the main show, *They Drive By Night*.

So let's see. By now I was somehow along the shaded back side of Guilder's, where I could peer around the corner. I was keeping an eye peeled on the road between the Sinclair station and the projection booth, for that was where I'd told Sandy Dehner I'd meet her: where I'd envisioned her pulling up in that gleaming red jewel of a Thunderbird I had seen briefly at Les Champs du Roi. Then I would stride out of my obscurity and, banged-up face or not, clamber briskly into the T-Bird, and we'd be off, leaving the swamp-rats behind to gawk and cough in our dust as Miller Springstead and his cutie-pie whizzed well beyond the pale of this dump of a town where inertia'd fought entropy and nobody'd won.

The go-buy-pop-and-junk light was still on, and a honky-tonked version of "Nola" began. And Leo Hanson was there beside me, handing me a Mason jar of his homemade cherry wine. I took a large gulp, keeping my vigil for Sandy, eyeing the place where she would arrive, that strip of road now occupied by half a dozen or so freshmen boys, callow, awkward as mantises, who scuffled mindlessly about, goosing each other ("Know how to play squirrel? *Grab a nut'n run!*").

I didn't know which I was more afraid of: that she wasn't coming or that she was.

*

Tuesday evening I had driven Turner's pickup over to Les Champs du Roi to pick up Rex, who was filling in as a temporary pot washer that summer.

I had gone early to steal a swim. All my life I'd swum at various spots on Silverfish Lake, but here, mincing along cement walks still warm from the overripe sun I had watched dip into the lake's western perimeter minutes before, I nonetheless felt an intruder—a feeling made even more acute by the litter on the long wooden dock I came to that arched gracefully as a bird's wing out over the gleaming water: towels, water-skis, canvas bags with airline emblems, books, boating paraphernalia I couldn't identify, lay strewn about like exotic refuse. On a bench near me lay a 35 millimeter camera, its fat lens gleaming in the dying light. I felt an impulse to grab the camera and haul ass wildly, screaming: "Take that you dirty rich sonsabitches!" giving them all the finger as I hot-footed it—

It wasn't a serious itch, but I stooped to at least touch and perhaps examine the camera when just by the dock's end a girl burst foaming up out of the water.

She grabbed the edge of the dock and hoisted herself vigorously yet gracefully onto the weathered wood. Her hair was slick against her skull and water cascaded from her black nylon tank suit to stain the gray dock boards the black of tarnished silver. With hearty movements she rose to her feet and stood before me, mere inches away. She was about three inches shorter than me, about my age and slippery-looking as an otter in her skin-tight suit. Water beaded on her Sea & Ski-scented skin as on waxed metal. Her face was oval, framed with perfectly straight blond bangs. She had a button nose with an upward tilt and eyes that in the failing light were a delicate blue, a peculiar, almost luminous shade somewhere between bleached cornflowers and silver; and in the meager light offered us as the last blood-red fingers of sun poked into tunneled black and gray clouds above us, they shone like coins.

"Who're you?" she asked in an arch, curious voice.

"Me? Uh, I'm Miller Springstead."

"Well, I'm Sandy Dehner, spelled with an aitch. All I can say is, I'm glad they finally got some younger people around here. I

73

guess a lot of kids have already started school. I don't go back to Country Day in Cincy for another week. I haven't seen you in the dining room. Are you a transient in the Lodge, or are you in a cottage?"

Before I even cleared my throat to answer, she chattered rapidly on: "The trouble with this place is, too many old people and too many people who just don't know how to have any fun. Anyhow, you just get to know people here and the next day or so they've gone back to Detroit or St. Louis or Cincinatti or wherever—that's where I'm from by the way, Cincinatti. Where are you from?"

"Ermine Falls," I croaked, my throat feeling gummy with the truth. "That's about six miles due east..." I seized hopefully on the sound of where I came from—maybe when you heard Ermine Falls you'd think of royalty's white, black-tipped robes, not of anything as commonplace as a weasel, a wily brown band— except when it was white in the winter—of lithe muscle and meanness that'd nip into your henhouse in the dead of night and rip the shit out of every feathered throat—

"Wow! Neat!" Sandy clapped her hands delightedly together: "You're a *local*," she bubbled, "oh, that's kind of rilly unique. I mean we just hardly see you people at all except for some of the kitchen help and the maids. Ermine *Falls*, I know where it is, it's that sort of nifty little four corners on the way to the airport in Traverse City. My mom says she's just *got* to go to that quaint old general store there before we go home. It was so funny, when we drove past coming here I saw a *cat* in the window. It looked like a sort of nifty place, like it probably had the most fascinating stuff inside..."

I thought of Guilder's dank and cavernous interior, redolent of ground coffee, drying leather, catshit, gun oil and cigar and vegetal essences slowly draining into static afternoons. Scruffy town kids would loiter inside, pawing aimlessly through racks of funny books as rolls of fly paper uncoiled slowly above them.

"What's your name again? Just your first name is okay."

"Miller."

"Well, Miller, what do you do for fun around here?"

I looked directly into her guileless, enthusiastic eyes, and for half a moment I felt like telling the truth: Oh, we get drunked up on homebrew or Stroh's or muscatel if we can find somebody to

74

buy, we fart around with cars a lot and go tear-assing around on dirt roads, we work plenty, we go hunting and fishing, we pick potatoes in the fall and cherries in the summer, Morel mushrooms in the spring, when we turn sixteen we try to get a job at the cherry cannery in Elk Rapids in the summer. We pull our porks a lot and get what we can, which is usually at best a little stinkfinger in the back of the bus coming home from basketball games...

"I mean," Sandy urged, "don't you have, oh, cakewalks and square dances and stuff like that up here? You know, all that kind of rilly unique stuff the boonies are known for?" She grinned for the first time, revealing large white teeth which conspired with faint traces of pink lipstick to give her a precocious, snottily sensual look. "Huh?" she prodded.

"Yeah, well, they have some of those things all right. Not now though. But they do have these free shows every Friday in the summers," I said, "the next one—the last one—is this coming Friday..."

"Free show? Day after tomorrow? Neat! Sort of like a little country flea market or something where country people sell you jams and jellies and native handicrafts and things?"

Flea market? "Oh," I said, "it's just a regular movie show only it's outside—the stores pay this guy to come show it and all the people come in from the hills and buy a lot of ice cream and pop and stuff... they all bring blankets and everybody flops down in that lot by Guilder's, or they line their cars up on either side of the booth, that's the thing that looks like a fish shanty on stilts—"

"—Oh *neat!* Can I come?"

"Sure," I said stupidly. "They're free."

"Oh, great, why don't we make it a date then? I can get the T-Bird on Friday I think, yes, I'm sure Daddy'll let me have it. Where'll we meet? You can show me all around, huh? Listen, right now I feel like another little swim, want to race me out to the diving raft?"

Maybe a time comes upon you when sucking hind tit ain't good enough any more and you just seem to have to plunge helplessly after what's retreating from you.

"You're on," I said, but she was already airborne and arching out over the darkening water.

75

*

"Here, your turn again, Miller."

Leo Hansen handed me the new third-full jar of syrupy cherry wine as I kept my eyes on the patch of road where Sandy would likely appear—if she did at all.

The lights above the projection booth had dimmed and a Porky Pig was in progress. The freshmen lingered in the road nonetheless, grab-assing, hooting, making fart noises, their voices alternately falsetto and croaking. They tilted their heads back on gawky necks to squirt thin streams of cigarette smoke arrogantly at the gleaming moon. It was as if they too were waiting for Sandy.

If they were still there when she came, I decided, lifted to a small plateau of optimism by my last mouthful of wine, I'd come among them like a weasel among chickens, scattering the bastards, then I'd triumphantly exit with my Sandy.

"Here, have 'nother belt of this panther piss, 'Stead," Leo said, and I took it gratefully, suddenly liking this thin blond boy with the lupine face; though not really my friend, we were nevertheless allies of a sort—we were the scholastic anomalies of Ermine Falls, both of us for some reason having an almost effortless facility with schoolwork.

The cartoon rattled on with explosive sounds and I heard the high-pitched gibber of cartoon animals locked in a struggle.

"What you lookin' for over there?"

"My snatch," I said. "Pretty soon this city snatch's gonna come get me in her T-Bird—you know, big-ass Thunderbird. She's just cuter'n a bug's ass, you'll see..."

"Do tell," Leo said politely. "Here, whyn't you polish this off, I'm gonna sneak back to the truck and boost my other jug—hey, *lookie there*!

And in the street, just where I'd imagined she'd be, she was: pulling slowly forward in her throbbing red dart of a car. Her hair had been shaped and styled so that when she turned her head, searching no doubt for me, it laggardly followed her skull's direction.

"Holy Jesus, you weren't shitting me one pound, were you, hell, Miller, go get'er, boy..."

I was already moving forward, unsteady from the wine and

76

cursing myself for having drunk so much of it. "Awright, fuckers," I muttered for courage, the words tickling my near-numb lips like carbonation, "outta the goddamn way, gonna show you how thish's done..." And I was moving forward awkwardly, lurching past couples necking on blankets, once stepping on an extended hand as Porky Pig's voice screamed behind me, "*Th-th-th-a-a-at's all, folks!*"

The harsh floodlamp over the booth came on as I approached the marvelous car, a sleek red Pegasus, its feathers and tail tucked in.

Sandy had already been accosted by the freshmen trash, who were leaning casually about on the glistening red metal.

"Hey, this here yourn?"

"How's come your daddy lets you out alone at night?"

"How's 'about we take us a little ride and open'er up, hey? Lemme drive, I'll show you how to wrap this thing around a corner..."

"Don't be so stuck-up, stuck-up, know what they say, they're old 'nuff to bleed, they're old 'nuff to stick."

"Hey, howdja like to meet the head of the fambly? Old Torpedo Number One? We could get in the backseat if they was one..."

My steps had slowed until I was barely moving. When I was within six feet of the car, I saw Sandy look around appraisingly: she was not at all afraid of her tormenters or admirers or whatever they were. Her eyes fell on me, then leaped into black holes of shadow as the intermission light winked off.

Just as my hand was reaching forward to jerk a couple of the kids away, her voice jumped out of the car at us, at me, like something fanged and clawed: "You *farmers*," she said with loathing and contempt. Had there been sufficient sibilance in the words, she'd have hissed them, she'd have spat on the ground had she not had manners.

I stopped dead as though a bullet'd nailed me in the breastbone, I began to back away from the car's hot penumbra of otherness, back into the sheltering dark—for surely had I reached her I'd have appeared no hero but merely another dreadful example of the hillbilly, hick, farmer, hayseed, swamp-rat, shit-kicker, posturing before her with his puffed face and Monkey Ward windbreaker and new jeans with four inch cuffs.

Tears sprang to my eyes as I steadied myself on a parked 39 Chevy, faintly rocking from the writhings of a blanket-covered couple within, and watched the beautiful resort girl pull away from Ermine Falls, Michigan, a look of disdain and disgust spreading on her still-not-entirely-formed face. In the background I heard the babble and scrabble of Laurel and Hardy's pointless hijinks; then one of the freshmen screamed after Sandy with a reedy, emphatic voice, just before she was out of earshot: "Up your giggy with a ten-foot pole, and 'round and 'round your ass-*hole!*"

Then another voice, the most quavering and callow of all, shrieked an obscene version of a much-used radio ad for drugstores: "Fuck you-all, from Rex-all!"

I slunk back deeper into the sheltering dark, awash with shame and drunkenness. And the fact that in the depths of my shame I found her to be as contemptible as myself and the rest of the world didn't in the slightest lessen my longing—if anything it sharpened it.

I began running the three miles home, and as soon as I got the chance I left the road and ran in the woods alongside it, my face and eyes continually lashed by branches which I seemed unable to see despite the brilliant moon overhead. Then somewhere a half-mile or so from home I fell on my knees to the punky floor of the woods and began to smash one fist after another into the soft ground, sobbing: *Nothing except pure pain is ever going to make me cry again, you sonsofbitches, you just see—*

*

Miller Springstead awoke with a start in Iowa City, face wet with the first tears shed for anything but hilarity and pain since he was eighteen. Scalding tears were blinding him as he rammed one fist after another into the spongy depths of his pillow.

Convulsed with sobs, he staggered to his feet and lurched to the window.

He looked up at the gleaming spider's egg of the moon, almost hideous in its clarity; now it seemed to be moving, pursued by scraps of black cloud lean as half-starved animals.

Once Turner'd told him: "It's a shame that sometimes things don't seem to get better as you go along—but at the least you can get a little smarter, and maybe that's all the edge things're going to give you, that don't come from pure luck, anyhow..."

Miller brushed his forearm across his eyes, but still they leaked, and his salt was bitter on his lips.

He blinked, hard, but continued to weep softly, so that prismed through his tears were moons upon moons: there seemed dozens, scores, perhaps, all the same.

After a time the tears diminished and a single moon reasserted itself in his eyes, cold, distant, glittering, indifferent.

Edge of Summer

—O remember
In your narrowing dark hours
That more things move
Than blood in the heart.

"Night," Louise Bogan

ONE

On a Monday afternoon in August of 1967, Lindsay Noel Springstead left her husband, Miller, in Iowa City and flew to northern Michigan where her parents had moved from Bay City when she was fourteen. After a few days as a freshman in the Ermine Falls school she'd fled to Ann Arbor to live with her aunt Roxanne where she had finished school at University High. Since then she'd only spent summers and vacations and odds and ends of time in Ermine Falls; nevertheless, it seemed to have suddenly become, with the crisis in her marriage, home again.

She needed almost desperately to see her father: Vernon Noel had always been able to if not entirely fix then certainly assuage her hurts, big and small, and had as well practically always given in to her on all matters of importance, though of course he reserved strict stewardship of some things to demonstrate he was still essentially in control.

Lindsay and Miller had been married in Petoskey a little over a year ago, and for a little while after they'd moved to Iowa City the wife of a graduate student at the University of Iowa had been a kind of fun role to play. At first, Miller'd seemed happy enough—relieved, perhaps—to be able to immerse himself in his graduate studies and the two sections of freshman rhetoric he taught as a Teaching Assistant, and she got a job waitressing at a place called The Colonial along the Coralville "strip." She had a B.A. in sosh from the U of M and as long as the waitressing wasn't serious, it was fun enough, not to mention being the only thing she really knew how to do well. In fact she'd been waitressing last summer at Ermine Hills resort in Ermine Falls when she had met Miller and become engaged to him.

But then after a while, and who knew exactly when this phase began, probably sometime during the early part of the brutal winter, it wasn't much fun anymore, in fact *everything* began to seem like real work and they found themselves drudging along for who knew what exactly except for Miller to do his course work and get prepared for and then through his comprehensive exams for his PhD (*Comps!* the very word sounded evil, like *cleaver*). Then there was the matter of a dissertation.

She had been reviewing her many charges against him on the plane from Cedar Rapids to Chicago but it was all making her very tired—maybe because she persisted in not thinking of what had really precipitated their last quarrel, which was that she'd very recently committed—this was a word she couldn't, wouldn't, say aloud, could barely think—adultery with a boy—no, man— she'd known at the U of M who had been a friend and fraternity brother of her first real lover, Royal Bergeron. And there had been no fun at all attached to any of it. Randy Wilder'd turned up as a part-time manager at the Colonial and as a student at the Iowa Writers' Workshop: and somehow she'd fucked him or he her—some aspects and reasons concerning the event were still obscure to her. But it hadn't been lust. Or not exactly. And much—maybe most—of it had been Miller's fault. Or so she kept telling herself when she could bring herself to think of it at all.

In the middle of her catalogue of complaints against Miller, a device that was working pretty well so far to keep her mind off her episode with Randy, she fell asleep to the drone of the Boeing 707, her head lodged loosely between the seat and cabin bulkhead, and found herself dreaming of that soft evening around eight o'clock a little over a year ago when they first came to Iowa City.

"We're home," Miller was saying as he switched off the truck, and in her dream she was just as sleepy as she'd been before she'd fallen asleep in the plane.

She looked through the cab of the U-Haul truck they'd driven from Michigan, towing their wedding gift Volvo station wagon, at the little green raised ranch perched sprucely on its basement and garage which were built into a sort of bank and thought drowsily, Gee, I bet I can live here...

She rolled her window further down and listened for the faint stirring of the elm on the median in front of the sidewalk running past their house. Sure enough, she could hear the sound of moving foliage and of crickets and various keening insects and nightbugs.

Miller reached over to massage her shoulder. The engine clicked and tinkled as it cooled.

"This is home," Miller said quietly.

"Well, let's go in, then I want to make some coffee, that's the first thing, and we can have kind of a picnic, there's lots of stuff left in the cooler—"

"Easy there, chickenwing." She could sense him grinning in the gathering dark. "There's no electricity yet, and probably no water. I'll get the juice turned on in the morning. I'll see, maybe I can figure out how to turn on the city water myself.

"Oh." She was achey and tired and this minor frustration after the prospect of making coffee in her—their—own house made her jaws ache. She was out of sorts anyhow from the trip from Michigan, two solid days of dreary jouncing in the rented truck, leaving Michigan for Wisconsin, Wisconsin for Minnesota, Minnesota for Iowa...

"Hey, c'mon, cheer up, Lindsay. Let's go in, I'll carry you across the threshold just like in the movies, I'll light the fire, we'll have a warm beer or two and relax before we start to move the stuff in..."

"Okay..."

There was a little wind behind her knees when Miller scooped her up under the legs with one arm and clutched her tightly to his chest with the other; it took him some moments, holding her thus, swaying, to unlock the door.

The door swung noiselessly back and they were inside, the house's dim interior looming emptily before them, cool, alien...

And empty! Though the close air was as yet little stirred by cooler night air just now flowing in through the screened front door, Lindsay breathed it happily.

"Not too bad for twelve grand spot cash, huh? In a way I hated to sink all the old man's insurance money and what I got for our property into one place, but hell, she'll be worth double that in a few years...this place is now our capital, so to speak...you think it's okay?"

"Yes, oh, I don't know, it's *dark* in here." She suddenly realized how really tired, sweaty, odorous, crabby, she was, she wanted a shower and she realized with a sense of panic that there might not even be water for going to the toilet.

Suddenly she felt sad and bit her lower lip, ready to weep: it

85

was like she was standing, waiting, on the platform of an empty train station. "Miller, something seems sort of funny in here..."

"Yeah? What? I could use a laugh or two."

"No, I mean how it seems in here with no lights and no furnishings. Listen, doesn't it sort of *ring* in here?"

"Yeah, maybe it is a trifle spooky, tell you what, wait here, I'll get the flashlight and see if I can turn the water on downstairs first so at least we have cold water tonight. Just wait—I'll be back..."

Alone, she sighed. Wait? Where would she go? She was tired from riding in the truck all day, had a headache from reading roadmaps ("You're the co-pilot," Miller'd said), and she realized there were hours—hours—of work, she would have to pack and tote like a coolie while Miller handled the big stuff like the stove and refrigerator from his family home in Ermine Falls that he'd sold to buy this place. It could all be fun if she weren't so tired and cranky. She slumped down before the fireplace, feeling a complete wreck in her dusty jeans and MSU beer jacket. And now she did have to go to the bathroom.

As if in answer, there was a mechanical groan from downstairs, and she could hear the gurgle and splash of water, then the sound of it surging and filling the pipes. "Guess who?" He had come up behind her from the stairs to the basement; his hands were firm and cool and slightly wet over her eyes. She lifted her hands and held his wrists.

"The Phantom of the Opera? How come your hands are wet?"

"All misanthropes have 'em, y'know..." His hands slid away from her eyes, her fingers slipped from his wrists. He pointed a flashlight into the fireplace: "Notice the fire, forethinkingly laid by me, back in June. Go ahead, light it."

She took matches he handed her and lit the wads of newspaper under the kindling. The kindling caught and began to ignite the logs.

She lost herself in the fire for a time, how long she did not know, but when she looked around again the logs were burning steadily and Miller was sitting beside her, regarding her curiously. "So you would've laid this fire about a week after you met me—we'd been going around together for a week and then you came out here for three days...so tell me, what were you thinking when you laid this fire? Were you figuring on asking me to marry

86

you when you got back? 'Cause that's when you did..."

"You ain't as dumb as you look."

"Oh yeah? Take this!" She jabbed him in the ribs with an elbow. She didn't have to go to the bathroom yet after all.   He easily wrestled her supine until her head was little more than a yard from the crackling fire; she arched against him, writhing, the flames hot against her face. Some damp strands of hair got caught in the corner of her mouth.

He leaned more forcefully over her to quell her movement. She butted her head into his face.

He bit at her hair, got a mouthful, gasped, got a better purchase, and tugged.

"Yeeow!" She squirmed under him, jerked her hair free, twisted to bite at his face, kissed him instead, surprising him into slackening his grip. She did not take advantage of him.

"Mah little chickadee."

"You getting much these days, swamp-rat?"

"Not as much as I can handle—Jesus, nice mouth, who you picking your bad habits up from?"

"Mmmmmm?" And they began to claw off their clothes and hurl them carelessly into the room's emptiness and soon, as the flames cast queer writhing shapes on the walls in the semi-darkness, they made sweaty and forceful love, their bodies slick and their odors rich in their nostrils. For a few moments Miller sucked a spot on Lindsay's shoulder as though it were a sweetened lime. As they grew quick-breathed and slimy at their juncture and were achieving new heights of orange tickle and rub, Lindsay was barely aware of Miller murmuring something about the softness of the insides of her thighs.

They were still joined and she fell into a sudden pool of drowsiness and well-being...then Miller left and she drifted, thinking, How warm the fire is, as green as grass, and then a pillow was put beneath her head and something covered her body and she could hear Miller moving about and it was oddly pleasant, the way you felt coming home from the movies and you're in the back seat and you hear your parents talking low in the front seat.

TWO

I rode the city bus back home from a pointless trip to the office at the EPB I shared with Seymour Shapiro, another Teaching Assistant—I had thought it might calm me a bit to sit at my desk in the late afternoon and perhaps read some passages from one of my or Shap's books, but sitting there had made me restless to get back and continue whatever was to be continued with Lindsay—only to find her gone; she was going back to Ermine Falls, her note said, "to think," and I could pick the Volvo up at the Cedar Rapids airport—probably, she noted, making plans for me even in her absence, I could get Shap or somebody to drive me there.

I was still a little drunk from two icy drafts at Donnely's and from saucing the night before after we had our argument that led to the present state of affairs...did I intend a pun? I had to restrain myself from spitting on the wall-to-wall carpeting of this "raised ranch," as real estate jargon had it. So I'd sunk the bulk of Turner's insurance on his own life—nobody had even suggested he was the suicide I knew him to be—and the sale of TURNER'S AUTO & TRUCK PARTS into this abode, and it was turning out not to provide the new start and be the love nest where I transformed myself into professor material and Lindsay and I made out like bandits at being nice young up-and-coming married folks, but...what? Call it Miller's Folly. I wondered what I might get for it, how long it would take to sell, how much of a beating I might have to take. And then I did spit on the god-damned floor.

There were a dozen cans of Budweiser left in the refrigerator and I drained two of them without shutting the door. I'd have to hike or ride my bike down to Jensen's Grocery a little later and replenish my supply, but first, I sensed I was, mercifully, fatigued enough in mind, body, and, if I had one, soul, so that I could probably catch a little sleep; so first, before whatever came next, I'd by God have me a nap—to knit up the old ravel'd sleeve of care, right? For all the good it'd ultimately do, since things would still be facing me when I awoke. Sleep is too short a death, as Weldon Kees said somewhere.

Lately in my dreams I'd been going further and further back. Why? To get some assurance there was, had been, a time without pain, anxiety, dread, and to know that it was actually possible to live at peace with yourself and the world? Or for pure escape, or was it just some vagary of memory I couldn't fathom?

I went into our bedroom. The covers were messily pulled up just as I'd left them before heading for my office—Lindsay must have packed her bag from stuff in the drawers and closet in a hurry, but nothing looked much disturbed; somehow it'd have been almost comforting if I'd found some things she in exasperation had hurled to the floor or against a wall. But that wasn't her style. And now no doubt she was traveling light, a rich kid's privilege—don't worry about the old stuff, Daddy'll spring for some new, since you'll always be his little girl no matter what.

So I flopped on the wrinkled bedspread, my head on a pillow, and covered my eyes with my forearm.

Maybe more to the point than seeking a point of innocence was seeking the point where you first became aware of something other than good intentions; when you first recognized the existence of cruelty, perversity, and what for lack of a better term you might call evil: when? Or was it all, finally, as Hamlet said, words, words, words.

I thought back to this same month, August, when I was five and Rex was eight. Behind my shut eyes I could see him trudging before me toward Sonney and Pearl's where we were staying while Pa was at the War—"Killing Japs," Sonney would say with an unaccustomed viciousness, the cords standing out in relief in his thin neck—and watching his new Monkey Ward tennis shoes raise puffs of dust.

I melted back into the mattress: I thought of what it felt like to lie on the thick shag of our lawn in Ermine Falls and look at the tops of the maples waving high above and feel as if I was sinking into the earth.

I wear my bib overalls like Rex. Pearl stands at the backdoor of the unpainted house, its light gray clapboards silvering. Pearl is spare, gray, smells like the house: camphor, sweat, kerosene, boiled cabbage.

She has ceased her potato peeling. A paring knife is clamped amongst the fingers of her hand as though it has grown there from a seed. She has two empty gunny sacks and our lunches wrapped in butcher paper. A sweating two-quart jar of lemonade sits on the stoop at her feet. Sonney is off helping John Hoffstettler hay on the adjoining farm. We can see him in the distance as he jounces along on the hayrake behind John's tractor, proudly erect on the seat over the rake's shiny curved tines.

"You young fellers'd best go over to that back five acres first," Pearl says. "It should be real good there."

We'd probably have headed there first no matter what: not proper hay any more, the plot contains whatever has managed by luck to root and thrive, Indian paintbrush, purple vetch, goldenrod, patches of clover, alfalfa, dill, and plenty of milkweed.

Pearl's eyes are bright in her spare weathered face; they fall upon us with clear affection. "You boys'll look back on this time one day and you'll be proud of having did your share, and your daddy'll be proud when he comes home. Sonney thinks it might end directly. So when you get them milkweed pods, you just think of one of our boys getting shot down by the Japs and then not drownding in the ocean because of his life jacket being stuffed with fluff made out of you boyses' pickins'..."

Rex takes up the gunny sacks. He hands me one and takes both lunches. I pick up the jar of lemonade and follow him.

As we leave the yard we hear the *thwack-thwack* of Pearl's wooden spoon as she mashes a dot of egg-yolk dye like a blood spot into a white lump of wartime oleo in a mixing bowl.

"C'mon Miller."

We walk toward the weed-glutted five acres across the stubble of a shorn hayfield. The dull slam of Hoffstetler's old John Deere to our left—*ka-thunk, ka-thunk*—is reassuring as a heartbeat.

We leave the stiff, sun-dried stubble and enter our acres. We have to slog and struggle through skeins of resisting vetch, through berry bushes, thistles, wild snapdragons, there are brambles, prickers, sand burrs; hosts of grasshoppers flee before us as do cabbage moths and an occasional monarch or tiger-swallowtail. There are all kinds of buzzings, honey bees in profusion, and every now and then a snoring bumblebee wobbles past.

On we push through the tenacious vines and crawlers, the

barbed berry bushes—nothing yields without some struggle.

Rex breaks trail straight for our lunch spot, a vast beech tree in the field's center.

Rex plants our lunch in the shade of the beech, I put the jug next to it, and soon we are hard at it, plucking the pods from milkweed plants and shoving them into the gunny sacks that smell of something strong as creosote, maybe last fall's walnuts.

Our hands become sticky as flypaper. Later, when we go back, Pearl will come out on the porch and will help us shuck away the pods and get at the insides, delicate, like some kind of unborn birds, which we'll put into sacks to be taken into Guilder's later on and sold for fifty cents a bag—we will save the money in a jar until we get enough to buy a Savings Bond.

Recalling what Pearl said, I see a fighter plane with a circled star on its side ditching in the ocean, an aviator with helmet and goggles leaping from its wing before it is swamped—it is our father, Turner, and he is miraculously buoyed up by his life jacket—

—Rex drops a milkweed pod down the front of my bib, and it drops instantly to my crotch—I leap into a crazed dance of fear, sure it is acrawl with wasps, yellowjackets—

As Rex giggles and snorts at my predicament, I thrash wildly about, claw my overalls down enough to hurl the crushed pod away. "Boy, you're gonna get it," I say poisonously, "I'm gonna kill you." And I head for him, legs churning as I try to hitch up my overalls.

It is no use, he easily outdistances me, and by the time we circle back to the beech, I am so tired I forgive him for now, resolving to get him one way or another on the way back.

We flop beneath the tree. Its huge roots are above ground like monstrous veins and Rex has fitted himself into a natural chair they form. "Want some lunch?" He offers me my sack. "Don't hog that," he says as I reach for the lemonade.

I take a long scornful swallow, then bite into a sandwich made of the rough heavy bread Pearl makes and fried pork and mustard.

Rex eats with one hand and plucks sand burrs from his cuffs with the other. He rises, chewing noisily, and points with his half-eaten sandwich: "Lookie there!"

A buzzing spot in the sky is coming toward us—a light

airplane, and its wings waggle cheerfully as it comes into full view and the angry bee-buzz of its engine grows.

The plane circles our field, banking around it in swoops as gracefully insolent as a crow's. Whoever is in the plane is clearly happy.

"Maybe that's the Japs who won the war and're coming to get us," I say.

I will have to be scarier than that to get Rex's goat: "Naw," he says, "it's just some of them resorters fooling around and showing off."

The little plane gives a last foolish waggle of its wings and flies off...pursued, or so it seems, by huge dark clouds that have appeared suddenly in the west. Black fingers reach through the sky's tender blue like the residue of some great explosion, and as the spreading dark stain in the summer sky drifts toward us, the air grows dank, like before an electrical storm, and the scents of milkweed, hay and mustard rise around us.

Rex licks his fingers and wipes them on his bib. "You reckon Pa will get back okay from the god-danged war?" he asks.

"Sure." I try to summon him up in my head, but can hardly remember what he looks like.

Dark clouds are merging above us, soon there will be rain, and as I look up into the eye of the storm I say, "Sure, you damn betcha, Sonney says the Japs are losing."

I feel the first drops of rain fall on my face and I look down to see Sonney striding rapidly through the overgrown field toward us, moving faster than I've seen him move in a long time, and he is crying out a word I have never heard: *"Hero-sheema!"* he calls out as he advances, *"Hero-sheema!"*

*

Now how the hell did I get here?

I am lying face down, someplace familiar.

I roll over on my back. My forehead aches and feels bruised. I roll to the right.

Aha! Somehow I have ended up on our carpeted bedroom floor. From where I am I can roll my head and look under the bed: venerable dust bunnies tremble from my breathing, I spot an old Tampax casing, a *Time* magazine, a pair of Lindsay's lime-green

92

panties with Saturday stitched across the front, the crotch stained the color of clover honey. I touch them and their silken, wet-mink feel is enough even in my depleted condition to give me a roaring hard-on: ah, Lindsay, I suspect you was just another trick of those mad and malevolent gods that make the gears turn all through the night, but god you were—are—delectable. But another trick indeed: for a taste of you was just the gods' way of saying, See what really might have been? If the both of you had been up to it?

Then I see something else under the bed: a Victor mousetrap clamped across the corpse of a small mouse, its mouth with its tiny teeth in a rictus of agony a fraction of an inch from a bit of dried cheese on the trap's tongue. Hello, there, brother, sorry for your misfortune.

Lindsay got hysterical about mice in February when she'd seen one nip into the bedroom closet: "Miller, get them out! Oh God, I can stand a lot of things but I can't stand rats!"

"It's just a mouse, Lindsay, for Christ's sake, thought I saw a bit of white on him, probably just a meadow mouse from outside that blundered in—he's sure scareder than you are."

"Well, *do* something! Kill it!"

"I can probably get rid of any mice we got...but if you want me to kill them in the process, do it yourself. I don't like killing things—animals, anyhow, I reckon a human'd be a whole other story..."

"*Coward!* You just do it! You're supposed to—that's your job, isn't it?"

"What? Killing things?"

"*No!* Being a *husband!*"

I was still laughing—in retrospect not a smart thing to do— as she flounced out the door to go buy some traps.

I couldn't stop myself: "And be sure you get some rat cheese too!" I yelled after her through my tears of mirth.

*

Lindsay is back, has set her three traps, one under our bed. She is incensed at having to deal with this herself. After she has done so, we face each other in the arena of the living room. Surely this is for the delectation of mad wheel-turning gods somewhere.

93

"Provincial!" she hisses. "Schmuck! I work my *ass* off as a waitress, I won't take any money from Daddy because of your stupid pride, I try to be a good wife, and when I expect you to do the things a husband should—"

"You don't understand—I don't want a *wife*...I mean,what a wife *is*, I mean normally, you understand, an empty-headed dependent you support to wash your drawers and iron your shirts, I...want us to be partners in this here enterprise I thought we were trying to build...I want you to get some plans beyond being little rich girl play-acting at waitressing or becoming Mrs. Professor, assuming I can pass my comps and then do a dissertation and then eventually actually find some shithole that'd hire me to teach their youth...I think *you* oughta go to grad school, frankly, I want—"

—"Hateful! You *want*, you *want*! Who gives a shit *what* you want? *Play*-acting at being a waitress? Listen you asshole—"

*

I find myself sitting still on the bedroom floor, but now with my back braced against the bed. Somehow I have removed the mouse from the trap. Its tiny corpse has long since desiccated to near weightlessness and I hold it by its stiff tail. I bring Lindsay's panties to my face with my other hand, sniff them, but smell only must, dust, nothing to re-create her.

I drop them and hold the mouse a few inches in front of my eyes: "Why hello there, ole brother under the fur, how's 'bout me'n you we have us a li'l toast...well I'll be god-damned!" By luck one of the several beer cans around me is fairly cold, though I can't recall having got up to get it.

I glance at the clock on the dresser. Somehow it has got to be six o'clock. I bring the can close and drain it, still looking at the mouse. Have to get down to the store soon.

I get up and lurch out to the living room. I take a good-sized chunk of oak firewood from the wood holder, sweep the fireplace screen aside, and set it up horizontally in the fireplace.

Then I thumbtack the mouse by its tail to the chunk of wood.

94

THREE

Lindsay descended the ramp of the wretched tooth-rattling North Central Airlines propjet that had brought her from Chicago to Traverse City by six o'clock. Something about the Traverse City Airport startled her; perhaps it was the smallness, or perhaps the memory it elicited: she'd not been here since— when? Not since she'd flown to St. Louis winter before last when she'd spent most of Christmas vacation with Royal Bergeron and his family, just after they were pinned and it seemed fairly likely that they'd get engaged and maybe even married when they both graduated from Michigan.

Everybody, from airline personnel to rent-a-car girls, seemed to dawdle over their tasks, as if that was your strategy for passing time when you were in the sticks.

She rounded a corner of the terminal and found herself half-talking, half-weeping, into the lapel of Vernon Noel's candy-striped blazer of delicate saffron interspersed with mocha. "Oh what a godawful trip," she moaned.

"There, there. Welcome back to God's country, sweetheart."

*

The hopeful odors of carpeting and new upholstery rose around her in the sparkling new black Olds and Lindsay began to feel better from the steady chill breath from air-conditoner ducts and almost ready for whatever might be waiting for her at home with her mother and Bertha, their cook-maid-and-bottlewasher, as her father'd often said (out of Bertha's presence)—*ugh* for Bertha, that stolid whiskery old bitch with whom she'd been in contention since she could remember, first in Bay City and then in Ermine Falls after her father brought—"forced," her mother liked to say—them north: square face, pursey mouth forever pinched in disapproval, tight gray curls bunched like grapes above her low forehead and dour countenance.

"Maybe I better tell you before we see your mother, kiddo, but you look like hell...'course I know it's been tough lately...Milt was going to come with me but at the last minute he got trapped with something on the main lift, you know how he dotes on you. Turns out the damn lifts break down more from sightseers in the summer than skiers in the winter...we're both tending to think God's Country is beginning to get a little cluttered—Christ, you should see some of the monkies who swarm in from Detroit and Pontiac and Muskegon. Very, very low class, all these rubes dragging in from oohing and aahing over Mackinac Island with their damned boxes of Doug Murdick's fudge—well look! It was gray before, guess you brought a little of that Iowa sunshine with you..."

Indeed the sun had come out from behind gray clouds—she could almost feel it as it fell through the tinted windows.

Her father was looking at her strangely through lavender teardrop sunglasses with gold frames and she suddenly noticed the difference she'd so far only sensed: Daddy'd lost weight—a lot of it. He'd been hefty all his life, vacillating between 210 and 240, but now his paunch ("Diet? Dye-it?" went one of his oldest jokes: "It's the *shape*, not the color of the damned thing!"), was for the most part gone, as were the chest deposits that used to give him a slightly breasted look. She could only guess the effort this must have cost him, for she knew his passion for the elaborate sundaes with whipped cream in Byzantine spires that had been their shared passion during her pre-teen years, and on especially lovely summer evenings in Bay City they were often conspirators in late-night sallies upon the freezer.

Once, she recalled, Daddy'd quit smoking for a week, then started again because nobody, including Wyn, who'd often told him he should quit, had noticed.

Her mouth was dry; she parted her lips to compliment Vernon but he was already speaking: "I suppose you'll think it's kind of funny without Bertha around the house, but not to worry, Wynn's found a...a crackerjack replacement..."

"What? Why? What happened to Bertha?"

He looked at her strangely again: "Why, Bertha's dead, of course."

"*Dead*?"

"Well, Wyn told you—wrote you, told you all about it, at least she said she did...you sure she didn't, around about in...February? Early in the month?" His thinner mouth made him look fretful, pettish, a bit tired in some fundamental way.

They were passing along a stretch of highway outside Traverse City touted in brochures as the "Miracle Mile, An Uninterrupted Mile of Pure Sugar Sand Beaches," which was more built up with motels and restaurants than she recalled. Small whitecaps dotted the green-black of Grand Traverse Bay, and splinters of magenta clung to the ropelike underbellies of clouds in the east.

"...when they were miffed at each other?" her father was saying. "How your mother'd go around shutting bureau drawers with a clump to let Bertha know who was boss and how Bertha'd bang things around in the kitchen? Well, turns out Bertha was in a snit because Wyn'd given her hell for—of all things—just folding and not *pressing* my undershorts when they came out of the dryer. As if it could have mattered to me. Anyhow, as per usual, I made myself scarce, and I guess what happened was, Bertha was in the kitchen and for some reason she was jabbing a fork into the toaster and, well, she got a hell of a shock, which touched off the coronary that killed her two hours later." A note of awe came into his voice: "Jesus, it was something...ambulance, flashing lights, stretcher, the works, like something on TV, something like that's enough to put the fear of God into you..."

"I'm sorry, Daddy...so sorry...oh, I'm a terrible person"—as she said it, she realized she was inexorably, as she had all her life, using the present circumstance to bring attention to bear on herself—"but it was awful working at the Colonial in February, God, Iowa was cold and gray and it was six days a week, I...just never opened any of Mom's letters that month so I didn't *know*, Daddy, and I just couldn't *stand* to use the telephone, I'm *so* sorry...oh, Daddy, I'm so happy you dieted, oh, you look so great, really you do, oh what's the matter with me, why am I so terrible? Is it because I was an only child like Mom thinks?" At last she could let herself go; it was ecstasy to let scalding tears flood her eyes, and she pressed her face against the gorgeous fabric of her father's clothes-horse's sport coat and bawled.

He looped his free arm around her shoulders and pulled her to him. Close as lovers they sped toward home. Purple tunnels engulfed the last shards of magenta above them.

Vernon Noel's voice was thick with love: "You're no kind of terrible person, believe you me, *I* should know. Now, no more of this depressing stuff: you're my girl and now you're home and we'll sort it all out later, and that's that."

Her face still slick with tears, Lindsay pressed into the lovely fabric covering his shoulder and stayed there without moving or making a sound. For the moment, it was almost as good as dreamless sleep.

"That's my girl. Rest."

FOUR

I sat cross-legged on the carpeted floor in front of our fireplace and stuffed the seventh round down into Turner's old—circa 1915—Steyr 9 mm pistol. It was kind of a curiosity: it had no clip and you forced the shells down into a magazine in the handle, keeping the action locked open by hooking the thumb safety into a slot on the slide.

When the magazine was full I took a last round from the box of old Austrian military ammo and pushed it into the chamber, then gripping the whole works firmly pressed the top shell in the magazine down and slowly released the safety and let the slide ease forward on the round in the chamber—it took care to not catch your thumb, and the slide had a strong spring. I let the hammer down slowly and put the safety on. Then I rested with my eyes closed and my head hanging down, breathing regularly, trying to keep things whole; handling weapons when you're three-quarters juiced is a tricky business.

Blam!

Without really realizing it I'd come out of my fugue, after a fashion aimed, and squeezed off a round: the fetor of cordite filled the room and the block of wood in the fireplace rocked back and forth, causing the dried mouse thumbtacked to the log to swing comically back and forth like a pendulum.

"Shit." I eased the hammer down, put on the safety, and put the gun aside.

I sought something to drink, poking among the trash on the coffee table, and was rewarded—a can of Budweiser half-full. It was warm but fizzed a little when I shook it and brought it to my ear. I drank it off and crawled to the couch, the big comfortable green corduroy couch Lindsay and I had argued over: I had been plenty pissed off when she'd spent a little bonanaza of $600 I'd got from a last insurance policy on Turner's life on a single sofa when we'd needed other things.

Well, it certainly didn't matter a damn now, and it was

surpassingly comfortable and cool on my hot cheek as I lay upon it and pulled a pillow over my head and thought back to a time Rex and I were ragging Turner in the shop, kidding him about going skating with us on Silverfish Lake, which happened to be prime for skating this second week of January of 1963, and we didn't want to waste the opportunity: there was a glaze slick as window glass under a fluffy four inches or so of snow which we could easily clear with pushbrooms from the shop.

"C'mon, Turner, why don't you grub the mold and rust off your old skates and sharpen'em up and we'll go on out a little 'fore lunch?" I suggest.

Turner is at the big vise on the bench—he has a set of Model A shift forks in it and he's using a triangular file on something. "Ah, you guys just want to watch the old man fall on his ass," he says, then is silent as he uses the file to probe a cavity in the forks' housing. "'Course that's natural as a pig in shit, I reckon," he muses, as if to himself. "It's nothing short of natural to want to see the old man get cut down to size every now and then...which is how it ought to be, I expect..."

He looks up and directs his gaze out through one of the dingy, nearly inpenetrable windows above the bench, out toward the road where we put up a stockade fence last summer when I came home from graduation at Central State. By now the unfinished cedar hiding much of the junkyard from Highway 31 has achieved a soft gray patina and is almost pretty. But Turner's fullest gaze, I know, is reserved for whatever is going on inside his head. College-wise now, I quote to myself a passage from Thomas Wolfe I memorized when we read *Look Homeward, Angel* in The American Novel: "Which of us has looked into his father's heart? Which of us has not remained forever prison-pent? Which of us is not forever a stranger and alone?"

Suddenly Turner turns his head, his eyes fall on me with clear affection and pride—I think—and he says, "You know, it eases my...conscience or whatever you want to call it that they's a Springstead graduated from college, and no matter how satisfying the grease-monkey way of life can be for his old man, he can maybe go out and do a few other things in the world...yeah, what the hell, maybe I ought to clean up my skates and show you guys how she's done, hell, I ain't had skates on in going on twenty years but like I was trying to tell you once upon a time, Miller,

100

once you get a real handle on something enough to make her a part of your whole self, well, maybe she'll stand you in good stead if your flesh ain't all gone to hell or your head addled."

He ceases fiddling with the transmission forks and brings his full attention to bear on the pair of skates I unearthed from the attic earlier in the day and that are now lying on the bench. The blades are brown with fine rust and there is a chalky fur of mold over the leather parts. But they seem sturdy, whole, and like him, most serviceable.

Suddenly I notice Rex looks a bit hang-dog for having been left out of the exchange.

Turner takes the skates over to the bench grinder, which has a wire brush wheel on it. "Go get me that can of neat's-foot-oil under the small bench, will you?" he says to Rex.

*

Naturally Rex and I scrambled from the pick-up, got our push brooms and hockey sticks and bulled our way out onto the ice while Turner had a leisurely cup of coffee from his thermos, then took his time putting his skates on in the cab while he listened to the local news on the radio.

And so after we'd lathered ourselves a bit in our crude variation of hockey, Turner walked to the lake in the snow on his skates...and moved slowly out onto the ice where we'd cleared it of snow.

But then instead of wobbling out on shaky ankles like I had expected, he came floating toward us like a ghost, hands thrust deep in the side pockets of his mackinaw. He swept past us slowly without greeting or even acknowledgement, and moved out toward the center of the lake following a thin wavering line of glassy ice the wind had blown free of snow, away from our raucous hoots of wonder and approval, graceful as a crow banking through a summer sky. Occasionally he reversed himself and skated backward, but with the same dreamy control, and for half a second I almost hated me and Rex because earlier we would not have believed his grace unless we saw it for ourselves.

101

This time I awakened slowly, as though swimming up from a great depth through murky water, perception coming by degrees: house, fireplace, mouse, myself on the rug, myself bereft, myself alone, myself. Myself, the word a curse.

Far back in my head was a fading vision of Turner silhouetted against the ice and snow, hands in his mackinaw pockets, watch cap over his ears, skating effortlessly into the void.

Then I thought of a time in summer; I must have been only seven or eight and Turner and Rex and I were out on the sandy plains in southeastern Skeegemog County where we picked huckleberries and I got a sweatbee in my ear: Christ! Thought I was going to die just from the racket—it was like having my head in a kettle drum being cut apart with a chainsaw, and I guess I went kind of crazy, thrashing around like a decapitated chicken until Turner got hold of me and held me firmly down on the ground. He poured tepid coffee from his thermos into my ear and floated the little bastard out, just like that.

I remember those big strong hands of his holding me so I couldn't scarcely wiggle and he just went ahead and took care of the whole troublesome thing in about two shakes.

I thought suddenly of Lindsay: where was she now, what doing, why hadn't we worked out, why had we got to such a pass—for her misery of spirit must have surpassed my own for this to happen—that she actually went and fucked a dipshit like Randy Wilder? Because he was from her home, or her kind of people, or where she really came from? Or because I had got so abominable through guilt and work and self-pity that she needed that kind of release? Could I absorb that as punishment and somehow call her back to my side?

Suppose we hadn't run off to Iowa: suppose we'd stayed right there in Ermine Falls, and I'd taken over the junkyard and run it and Lindsay'd stayed by my side...it seemed as impossible now as it had ever been, yet something about the notion haunted me. In any case, pointless though they probably were by this stage in the game, I didn't possess the power of mind to prevent such thoughts.

I thought I heard a whip-poor-will outside, then decided it was my imagination.

FIVE

Lindsay lay on her own bed in her own room swaddled in a heavy flannel robe of her father's she'd appropriated some years back. The room was dark and she could see the still faintly luminous borders of her glow-in-the-dark Bambi and Thumper pictures which she'd had ever since she was a little girl in Bay City.

She reviewed the last hour: she'd met Hilary, Bertha's replacement, a chunky round-faced local girl about her own age on whose short pale upper lip hovered an incipient mustache.

And of course she'd already had her first argument with her mother—she'd only needed to be in the house about three minutes for that to happen. At first Lindsay had felt maybe it wasn't going to be too awful because Wyn was dressed casually, in gray flannel slacks and a pink sweater. Wyn hadn't yet inquired into the exact circumstances of her daughter's return—delicacy would make her want to save that for later—and had been touting Hilary's virtues: "Hilary came to us almost by accident after poor Bertha was called away...what a comfort she was in those first awful days after Bertha was gone, oh, you can't imagine, Lindsay, you just can't *imagine*, how awful it is to have something awful happen in your own home, you can't im*ag*ine..."

"Yes, I can," Lindsay'd said and the battle was joined.

"Oh? *Can* you?"

Vernon had slipped away moments after depositing her and taking her single light suitcase upstairs—and Lindsay hadn't felt it a defection: for Christ's sake, let him get down to the basement to fiddle around in cool privacy with his power tools and maybe sneak a martini, she thought. He's entitled.

She and her mother stood at the foot of the stairs and Lindsay could not keep her eyes from longingly traveling the graceful upward curve of the staircase: the prospect of attaining the privacy of her room almost made her weak behind the knees; but as she put a tentative foot on the first carpeted stair, her mother had stepped briskly around her to precede and usher her forward.

"Don't you ever get out of jeans any more?" she asked over her shoulder.

"I wear a uniform at work," Lindsay said, climbing slowly, eyes on the stairs.

"Well, maybe you ought to—*oof!*"

Lindsay'd walked into her mother who had paused to speak.

"Well, watch where you're going, you ninny! Don't press *in* on me so!"

"Jesus...goodness," Lindsay muttered, stepping back.

"And please don't use language like that in my house, why the *idea*—oh!" Hilary stood at the top of the stairs holding a pile of towels and wash cloths stacked to her chin. "Hilary, dear, maybe after Lindsay's gotten freshened up a bit you'll fix her a cold plate of something, perhaps with some of that delicious roast beef from last night. I don't know just what you do to it but it's absolutely divine..."

"Just a little rosemary and marjoram and black pepper and garlic," Hilary said from the top of the stairs, peering down at Lindsay and Wyn as though into a well.

Lindsay and her mother attained the landing and moved past Hilary: "Now do get out of those ghastly jeans and jersey, Lindsay, I see you just brought a few things, but all the things you didn't take to Iowa are still there in your closet just where you left them...the light blue towels in the bathroom are yours, of course..."

"Thanks...Mom?"

"Yes?"

"Sorry I haven't written for such a long time, especially about Bertha and all..."

"Well, don't trouble yourself about that now, my dear, I gather from your presence here and now—and I won't say I told you so—and what little I've been able to gather from your father, you've got more...shall we say, *immediate* things to worry about. Now: whatever the problem exactly, and you don't have to tell me, I want you to speak frankly about it with the Reverend Arthur Dalyrimple whom I've invited for luncheon tomorrow at one sharp. He's a nice young Lutheran minister from Traverse City with considerable counseling qualifications and I believe it'd be best—"

"—yes, okay," Lindsay said, "fine, bring him on, but just now I've had the most wretched day and I've a splitting headache"—something about her mother always seemed to precipitate lies—"and I'm so tired I could drop and I just want to take a couple of aspirin and have a quick shower and maybe lie down for just a few minutes and let my nerves quit jangling, if you know what I mean..."

"How come you wear your hair all long and straight and lank like that, Lindsay? You could have such lovely hair. It's not quite as nicely reddish as when you were a girl, but it still has most of its auburn shade—you make me think of those hippies I think they call them that you see on the news all the time..."

"I'm really tired, Mom," Lindsay said, edging around her mother.

"Well, aren't we all."

And sure enough when Lindsay looked at Wyn's severe face in which spots of color were visible high on her delicate cheekbones, her mother was smirking her special smirk: Yes, it seemed to say, it's true, we're edging toward a collision, because I *want* to say I told you so again and again and I *will* say it again and again—

Lindsay's hand closed on a doorknob, but her mother suddenly shrilled: "Lindsay! Are you addled or something? That's not your room! That's ours! Whatever are you thinking? Why, yours is there, *there* where it's always been! And please don't take too long, will you, I don't like to keep poor Hilary here to wait hand and foot on us unless it's necessary: you see, she has to drive back to Skeegemog and do some things for her mother...I was so grateful to her when she stayed over in the guest room some of those awful dark winter nights just after poor Bertha'd gone...but our little family doesn't require her staying tonight, I shouldn't think. Do you?"

*

So Lindsay took a quick shower, put on her warm flannel robe, and lay down on her bed with a light blanket over her, and here she was. Her eyelids closed involuntarily—she really *was* tired—and a gentle cool breeze from the lovely Michigan evening scented with loam and dying blossoms wafted in from her

105

window, deliciously free of Iowa's oppressive humidity, and soothed her flushed skin, ("It's not so much the heat as the humidity," she heard an Iowa voice saying somewhere far away in the back of her head). She snuggled more into her robe—she'd always liked oversized hooded sweatshirts, maybe because they sort of enfolded you—and thought of Ermine Falls, and how she just now thought of it as home, now that she'd more or less run away from Miller, and their problems, and Randy and the whole thing. But how awful Ermine Falls had first been when she was thirteen and they moved here. Why had they moved anyhow? That was her father's fault, one of the few things she and her mother agreed on.

Gray flannel fingers of dream, ragged yet unrelenting, came for her: she was in the plane. Uncle Milton's plane. Milton Shelf really wasn't her uncle, he was Daddy's oldest and best friend and that was what she'd always called him. It was a single-engine Cessna. They were going up north, away from central Michigan and Bay City to the rugged North (as Daddy always said) and Milton was going to fly over where Ermine Hills was being built, a big ski resort which he was part-owner of and was going to run as soon as it was done. But she was cross and didn't understand why Daddy'd want to go north and make her and Mom move from where they were, there in comfortable Bay City. So Daddy wanted a bigger Olds Agency there in Skeegemog, the county seat. So he wanted to hunt and fish. So he claimed the north country was "God's Country"; and he didn't want to be away from Milton; couldn't stand his buddy moving away, so he was following him. Could it have been? So what: she and Mom liked it just fine where they were with their house in Bay City and their friends and Lindsay's school; she was just going to start her freshman year at Bay City Central when the roof fell in and Daddy said they were taking off like pioneers and going to live in God's country and wasn't that wonderful.

Bay City: their lovely big sprawling split-level raised ranch (which Daddy contemptuously called "splanch"); comfy and familiar and she was happy though she didn't know it during the pure tranquility of dolorous afternoons when she spent time around their pool and her parents' friends dropped by daily for cocktails and she might swim and dive and caper in her shiny black tank suit and later on go to her room and play her hi-fi,

106

stroking her arms as Harry Belafonte sang "Unchained Melody": "O my love...my darling...I've hungered for your touch..." Why should they go anywhere? It wasn't fair: they were where the trees, shrubs, roses, forsythia in their yard flourished from her father's ritualistic turning on of the sprinklers in the evening and in the dying sun rainbows would glitter around the sprinkler heads like the fabulous halos of flowers...and his Olds dealership: how about that, huh? Where on a sunny spring day you could gaze off across expanses of gleaming chrome and glass and terrazzo filled with sleek new Oldsmobiles; brilliant slabs of sunlight would filter lazily through the glass and the air would fill with scents of new car upholstery and freshly minted rubber. She could sit in her father's soft leather chair in his office and peer through a tinted glass wall at chipper young salesmen dealing with customers. Maybe everybody wasn't getting his money's worth, but if so nobody seemed to care.

The airplane: she was in back, Milton was pilot, Daddy sat next to him as if co-pilot, but he wasn't. Milton was thin and stringy, military, his oversized head of leonine white hair was swept back as though he were accustomed to plunging through the air at great velocity like some predatory bird.

Slyly she loosened her seatbelt and pulled a small pillow between her cheek and the fuselage and thus buffered, the plane's vibration became like a narcotic. She wore jeans and a heavy shaker knit sweater from Norway and a pair of calfskin jodhpurs her father had given her last weekend for the plane trip this weekend.

Sometime later she awoke sulkily and looked down, cross and, for the first time, despite the novelty of the plane ride, bored.

Her father had turned around and was saying something to her. "Rolly-coaster?" she asked, sleepy and grumpy.

"Haven't you always said you wanted to go on a roller-coaster?"

Now Milton looked back at her and she thought she could see him wink through one lens of his sunglasses. He made a signal to Vernon, an O formed by thumb and forefinger, and his strong hairy oversized hands fell to the funny half-wheel of the plane and they were falling.

The pit of her stomach rose until she was sure it was in her

mouth, like the slippery half of a canned peach she had once
swallowed whole on a dare and which had risen, whole, in her
mouth.

Worse than a sailboat heeling over, the ground thrust up at
them, trees that had looked benign as broccoli tops, houses and
cars like toys, all sprang up at her like fists.

Finally the plane leveled and her wits returned and they
were low enough to see people clearly and distinguish their
shirts and hats. For some moments they cruised nearly parallel
with the ground below. They began to climb as a huge steep hill
appeared and she saw a complex of half-built buildings. By the
biggest a man looked up at them, crossing and uncrossing his
arms in some obscure signal. They shot over him and climbed
again, but along the upsweep of the hill: there were craters and
raw yellow trails cut into the green and ant-humans and yellow
earth-moving machines moved comically about. There were
great sandy areas nippled with hundreds of stumps.

Her father, a bit ashen himself, turned to her again and
yelled over the engine, "You'll love it here in God's Country,
kiddo!"

He must have seen fright in her face: "Honest, you'll love it
here, Lindsay, and Wyn too—it'll be like being pioneers only
without the pain and inconvenience..."

He looked to Milton for reassurance and apparently caught
it through his friend's dark glasses, for they grinned at each
other the broad grin of men exhilarated by commitment to some
perilous undertaking.

*

And then she was dreaming about Ermine Falls and how she
came there as a freshman that fall...the school: ugly triple story
brick structure built in the 30s, tucked a few blocks off the main
drag, original yellow faded to something like clotted cream, that
housed kindergarten through twelve, a clutch of maybe seventy-
five students and half a dozen teachers, one of whom would be
Superintendent, one the Principal...

...the sounds even in her dreams now could cause a tremor:
clang: *bong*: chimey sounds from far out across the clayey yard
where elementary kids played, where they whirled about on

what they called The Giants, a metal pole from which handles hung down on chains. The idea was, you clung to one and propelled yourself around and around and around until you were so dizzy you had to fall off: and then the handles clanged against the pole and the chains jangled plaintively.

And how did I get there? I got there because of Daddy and Milton and that goddamned God's Country stuff: they sent me away to summer camp when they moved from Bay City to Ermine Falls and when Daddy picked me up to take me home it wasn't home any more, with my room and the pool and yard and all the flowers, they were all gone and now it was this new place, which was nifty I guess but didn't have a pool and smelt of paint and varnish. Daddy came to pick me up that Sunday morning near the end of August at Camp Rensselaer which he kept calling "Camp Rackrent" to be funny and we drove past the Saginaw Valley north to our new home in something over two hours with Daddy going eighty and kidding all the time over the dull FM Sunday music on the radio. I was really getting crabby as we drove through all these little towns that Daddy'd always called Whistle-Stops and One-Horse-Towns, and we pulled off into one and went down some side streets that hid some nice old houses but nothing to write home about and pulled up in front of this one that looked a little like pictures of Monticello and there on the porch were Mom and Bertha both grinning so I supposed Mom was a little drunk—

Clang. Bong. The school smelled of age and grunge and floor compound and those white things they put in urinals that the kids in Bay City called Polack Mints and chalk dust and pencil shavings...drying urine and cowflops, flakes of which were always on the floors from the boys' high-topped work shoes...

She dreamt on, her mind's eye flowing on as the Cessna had flowed over the northern Michigan landscape only now she was in the Ermine Falls school on her third and last day as a freshman there, still a bit stunned that this could really have happened, that she could really be *here*, not in Bay City, with her friends all clean and bright with names like Ashley Berenson and Jennifer Logan and Jim Huston and Kirstin Lowry and Daryles Hunicutt and Cydney Smythe and here she was amid all these wretched snot-nosed evil-smelling farm kids with names like Nuenschwander and Merilatt and Springstead and

109

Hoffstettler and boys who were already calling her stuck-up and Long Tall Sally behind her back. Sitting around her in study Hall was Beulah Horsenblatt all white-skinned and snuffing snot and Leo Hanson who looked like a little drunk lion and Etta Gibbon and Moe Undersuggin and Glorious Wadworth and a bunch of others whose names she hadn't learned yet...

Earlier in the day, though, she had tried out for freshman cheerleading and had become one—because Daddy urged me to, to "jump right in," he said. "Go ahead sweetheart, you'll do fine, don't look behind, as Satchel Paige used to say, you can't tell who might be gaining on you: just plunge right ahead into the thick of things and everything'll be just fine—you'll see." And so the afternoon of my second day I went into the sticky gym and the older girls who cheered the varsity squad who would vote on the younger girls were there and they gave me the stuff you had to wear: tacky black slacks that didn't fit and a loose orange sweater so you looked like a Hallowe'en doll. Evonne had helped me practice: you had to do turns and cartwheels and kind of a split and I got antsy as I waited for the frolicsome little twins named Francy and Nancy ahead of me and as I waited I felt a little nauseous and thought I was getting my period, but didn't think I could be, I'd had my first one at camp three weeks earlier where I'd had a little book and some Junior Kotex Mom had given me "just in case" but I was so scared and Jeanine my counselor came into the bathroom where I was all alone in a booth twitching and shaking because I'd just spotted and I knew what it meant and I was sitting on the stool sniffling and holding my knees together and trying to fix up that funny truss sort of belt and Jeanine who was a sophomore at Bennington and was kind of like the big sister I'd always wanted, ugh, who'd want to be an only child, she took me into a tiny room in the health center and calmed me down and got some vaseline and some little lubricated tampons and sat there on a turned-around chair with her trench coat on over her bathing suit smoking Chesterfieds and talked me into everything...now her dream wafted her into study hall: click: 3:02. And so now she was a cheerleader for the freshman squad, big deal, and was thinking how when Daddy'd taken her the previous night to see *The Horror of Dracula* in Traverse City she'd nearly vomited with fear and excitement at the part where Jonathan Harker gets done driving a stake into a beautiful

110

paramour of Dracula and after she's screamed and writhed with blood foaming up around the stake, he passes out, and then wakes up to drive a stake through Dracula, but Dracula's coffin is empty...it was 3:05. Some of the girls here didn't even wear deodorant. She wished the clock had a second hand. As she waited for 3:06, the second period of her life arrived a week early, a sudden flow presaged by little more than some seconds of wooziness: *O God...darn...*

Get up Lindsay, you've got to get out of here...

Her cardigan: thank God. As inconspicuously as possible, she stood up, drawing her sky-blue light wool cardigan from the back of her seat in one motion, pulling its arms around and tying it at her waist so the back covered her rear. She sidled toward the door, apparently regarded by no one, including Mr. Grebe, the science teacher proctor for this study hall, who was drowsing over the sports section of the *Detroit Free Press*, but nonetheless afraid someone would see a stain the size and shape of a splayed hand spreading on the cardigan and alarums would be sounded: she saw herself pursued, tottering along barely ahead of a host of boys who followed her like dogs after a bitch in heat, giggling and hooting and goosing each other, herself leaving little beads of blood shiny as nailheads on the waxed hardwood floors.

She gained the deserted hall and holding her breath she slipped past Mr. Mildwood's Superintendent's Office and then went slowly down the stairs, clutching the hand-polished bannister, her thighs wet and chafing.

She arrived unseen on the second floor. The only thing between her and the GIRLS at the far end of the hall was a hall monitor's station, a desk and a chair before a door to a storeroom where athletic and maintenance supplies were kept, a place reputed to be frequented by intrepid neckers—so Evonne had told her. Today it was manned by Basil Alewive, an 18 year old junior. He was pasty and beefy and squinted up at her through small recessed but bright eyes as she approached. He left off his reading of a funny book, *Tales From the Crypt*, and threw his leg into the hall to prevent her passing. She could smell cooking grease, tobacco, urine. Around the corners of his lips were a series of blanched little pustules that made her think of pancakes on the griddle before they're turned.

Echoing up the metal staircase behind her that led to the

furnace and pumproom and domain of the janitor where Evonne said kids sometimes crept off to smoke came a brief hot scrap of music from a radio, a throbbing voice, *Well just because you think you're so pretty*—then a distant door slammed quenching the sound.

"Where you pass?" inquired Basil, rising, closing his comic book. He was about her height, and not muscular but chunky and strong-looking.

Pass! She was supposed to have gotten a begrimed triangle of Masonite from Mr. Grebe with GIRLS scratched on it.

"Don't matter none," Basil said, "I'll get you 'nother, c'mon, I got extry in here."

Some twenty feet beyond him like some delectable oasis she could see the door to the GIRLS with its promise of a nickel machine and lots of tissue and cold water and a stall to be alone in.

But she followed Basil, adjusting her cardigan for maximum protection; she took four steps into the room and blundered in the gloom into a bundled wrestling mat; her legs collapsed and she sat down heavily upon the unresilient bulk of the mat. She could see a gymnast's pommel horse as if it were alive and watching her in the gloom.

She pressed her hands down to lever herself up, but there was Basil standing before her, rubbing a hand back and forth over the growing bulge behind his fly: this was the dream where your foot was caught in the tracks and the train was bearing down on you.

Basil's voice was rough, dry: "You think your shit don't stink?"

She said nothing. A plaintive gurgle of liquids around organs came from inside her.

"You wet your hair this morning?"

She didn't answer.

"What you do, piss through a straw? Hey, hear 'bout Johnny— he tells Teacher, Ma and Pa eat light bulbs at night, Teacher, she says, Why, Johnny, what *do* you mean? Johnny, he says, well, ever' night when they go to bed Pa says, 'Turn out the light, Maw, and let's eat it... hear 'bout Susie and Johnny, Susy, she tells Johnny, You know, Johnny, you fuck better'n Daddy'n Johnny, he says, I know, that's what Mommy says."

She felt cold as stone; the insides of her thighs were drying—from fear? she wondered remotely—but were damp and sticky.

Meanwhile, Basil was unbuttoning the top of his pants. "Here, stuck-up, want to meet the head of the family?"

Once when she was in the seventh grade she and Cindy Deforest had been visiting Bay City Handy and they'd snuck up to the door and eavesdropped on a sophomore girls' class entitled Personal Living and Hygiene but popularly known as "Sex Education," and listened to a Miss Price talking about the "sex act": "Preparatory to that, however, the penis becomes *engorged* with blood..."

And here was the thing itself, maybe the best thing on this stupid boy, vulnerable-looking, like a blind salamander.

Her hand was not her own: *she*, the *she* inside her was powerless to prevent her fingers from opening, nor to stay her arm from slowly starting to move the hand toward the indeed blood-engorged ever-stiffening member...or did it really move, would it have? To do what? Pet it? Caress it? Just touch it, gingerly, with a fingertip, like you might a corpse on a dare? She never found out because harsh flourescent lights flashed on overhead and as she shrank away from Basil, Rex Springstead, the handsome dark blade-faced temporary replacement janitor for Mr. Ouija who was in the hospital, moved briskly into the tableau beneath the light, making himself part of it—

Lindsay awakened suddenly, lurching up in bed, the sheets damp, falling away from her, her long U of M T-shirt she was wearing as a nighty wet with sweat under the flannel robe: it was dark in her room, all she could see were the glowing outlines of her Bambi and Thumper pictures, but cleaving her mind was the brightness from flourescent lights over nine years ago and there was Miller's older brother with a half-bemused yet flinty and all-comprehending look on his face, leaning casually on a pushbroom and sizing up the situation, then looking at once meanly and insolently into Basil's pasty countenance: "Well, well, well, what we got here..."

—I was stone, the only static thing in that room and everything else seemed made of gelatin, it was like something more than Laurel and Hardy, like the joke, Jimmy's got no arms or legs but that's okay, we can use him for third base.

She lay back, eyes shut: Rex in his OD trousers and T-shirt

113

moved toward herself and Basil, eyes hardening, and as Basil, head down, concentrated on stuffing his still-swollen cock back into his pants, Rex poised his pushbroom like a pool cue, big end toward Basil, and sighted down the shaft: Whop! Rex slammed the brush into Basil's face so he fell back against the wall, hands still scurrying to secure his fly, head nimbused with airborne grime.

As Basil pulled himself into some semblance of a boxer's crouch, Rex flipped his broom over his shoulder and bent his graceful brown neck forward in an almost Chaplinesque fashion to further assess this situation into which his janitorial duties had brought him; he looked at Lindsay, white with fear, cowering, pressing against the wrestling mat, and his almond-shaped eyes the color of creamed coffee lost their benevolant quizicality and became flinty; his voice came out low and very unlike the high, cajoling hillbilly tenor Lindsay'd heard him use with kids in the hall: "Well, Basil, ole pal, I do believe you've up and done her this time."

"You sonofabitch, Springstead, you ain't king shit around here," Basil muttered, eyes darting. "Me'n my girl want to mess around ain't no skin offa your prick."

"You'n your *girl*, huh, Sport? My crystal ball tells me I'm gonna see you squat your dirty ass down in Jackson Prison with your shirtails draggin' in the shit for what you're up to...I reckon ten years'd take some of the starch out of you..." He smiled at Basil, but there was no humor in his dark eyes. And suddenly she saw herself as Rex saw her: a new girl, a city kid according to his lights, innocently tripping along and getting waylaid and shunted into this cave for perverse Basil's foul purposes: for wasn't she truly terrified, aghast, cringing back against the mat in an access of shame, horror, embarrassment and fear; he'd have known nothing of the compulsion that had seized her hand and almost made it move—

The funny thing was, even at that moment she knew neither Rex nor Basil guessed at the real distress that had brought her here. Rex said to her almost timidly, looking as if he wanted to pat her shoulder but was afraid to, "You okay? You'd best come with me, now, and if the Super ain't in we'll get the Principal..."

"You do, I'll tell'em she was lettin' me play stink-finger with her!" Basil cried, in tears, just before he dodged past Rex and out

114

of the room. Rex didn't bother with pursuit.

The last bell rang conclusively through the hall, the sound of tramping feet grew, and somewhere a radio was turned on: Little Richard screamed, *Long Tall Sally's got a lot on the ball—I don't care if she's long and tall!*

"C'mon," Rex said, "we'll go see Missus Tattersall and set this thing into gear..."

Lindsay leaped from her bed, and stood on the braided rag rug by her bed, trembling; her robe slid to the floor and she tore the damp clinging T-shirt from her and for some moments stood nude and goose-pimpled, her arms crossed over her breasts as for protection. Then she picked up the robe from bed where it'd fallen and got into it. Instantly she felt better. She remembered how she'd persuaded Rex that no, all she wanted to do was go home, would he help her get away without anybody knowing?

She didn't tell him if he'd help her, sort of run interference so she could exit by the fire escape, that she'd already decided she would never again set foot in the Ermine Falls Community School for any reason, ever. No, never.

She wasn't sure how at that point, but she was sure she could fix it up with Daddy.

SIX

—We are going ice fishing: Turner moves on ahead of us on the frozen crust of iced snow over Silverfish Lake, a dynamic fleck in the otherwise static landscape, flaps turned down on his red plaid cap, mackinaw buttoned to his chin, clouds of breath rising like cartoon balloons, tugging the sled loaded with kindling and some coal, the minnow bucket, our fishing gear: and behind him come Rex and I, teen-agers, roistering in the chill northeastern breeze, hooting though no sound seems to come from us, clownishly grab-assing and poking each other until we are out of breath, yet bumbling ever forward...on Turner goes, getting smaller and smaller no matter how hard we try to catch up to him, and all of a sudden we are pursuing him in earnest, no more goofing around, but on he goes, oblivious to our pursuit, the only bit of movement in sky, snow, ice, until he finally either merges with it or somehow disappears on his own, leaving us behind, confused, and now we are suddenly breaking through the frozen shell and into the foot or so of wet snow beneath, our clothes have become heavy and sodden, my limbs don't seem to work right, our teeth chatter in fear and cold and we can offer each other no comfort—

I wake on the opened Hideabed in the little bedroom just to the left of our front door as you enter: the "study" we rather grandly named the room the night we moved in. We set up bookcases with my and Lindsay's books, and my desk and typewriter.

*

And now the dream from which I have arisen draws me back, bids me to consider again the last time I saw my father as he stood beside my idling VW to say goodbye to me—I was heading back for Mt. Haven to go to work in the Writing Lab for comp students in trouble that the English Department had set up. It

116

was early March of 1966.

Initially, I think I may even have congratulated myself on being able to assimilate Rex's death and keep on with my studies, as well as continue my efforts at getting a teaching assistantship at Iowa—I'd already been admitted to the grad school—and thus maybe find the channel to the next thing; maybe—and this only occurred to me weeks after Rex's death— the way Turner cracked up and wept that day after Rex's death deadened some nerve ends, allowed me to repress things so I could keep, at least for a time, going on without any visible fissures. Later in Mt. Haven I found a line in *Tender is the Night* that seemed designed for me: "The manner remains intact after the morale has shattered," the hero, Dick Diver, observed without irony of his own well-advanced process of disintegration.

And of course there was my rage: for a time I concentrated on hating mindless Dunstable, murderer of my brother, and I didn't let myself be too distracted by just how much Rex and I might have had to do with bringing disaster down upon our drunken foolish heads, but passed time hatching a lunatic's various murder and revenge schemes, ranging from ways to poison or electrocute Burner right up to blatantly drawing down on him with Rex's .300 Savage deer rifle with the Weaver scope, getting him in the crosshairs, and blowing his fucking brains out. Was my heart truly in it? I cannot tell.

Still, I could have stayed with Turner had he, after that first night, seemed any different: if only his hair'd turned stone white and he'd developed a stoop or a tic or something. But there he was, a little less talkative than usual, but otherwise moving the same, accepting what condolences were forthcoming; he was gentle with Sonney and Pearl who'd doted on me and Rex from the early days while they'd taken care of us first while Turner was off on benders and then during the war and then later in the early years when he was struggling to get the farm turned into a junkyard and get things humming enough to make a living.

Anyhow, on that last day, Turner leaned toward me through the window: "You take her easy to college and stop on back when you get a chance." He held out his hand. It was dry, hard, but seemed without force. Keeping myself together as carefully as I'd hold a handful of broken glass, I said, "Keep a tight asshole, Pa," what he used to tell me sometimes when I left for school, something he'd said he and his Marine pals used to tell each other before they went into action. For a crazy second I felt like I was the father and he was the son. But I had to go, had to; I backed out of the driveway and drove off, not letting myself look back and see Turner walk to the shop lest I fully grasp what I felt the degree of his loneliness and my desertion had to be and return myself, never to leave again.

*

Turner'd given me two hundred dollars for no particular reason—except to say it was left over because he wasn't going on his annual gambling expedition to the UP this year—and so back in Mt. Haven I didn't bother getting one of the stark little garrets I usually looked for but instead got an efficiency apartment in one of those electric-gadgeted apartment buildings with thick carpeting and the smell of new paint that'd begun to sprout like mushrooms in the town. I worked hard in the writing lab, extending myself mostly for athelete dunces who had to improve their writing skills. I drank little, drove aimlessly around town a lot, got Dr. Tyler to write a recommendation touting my teaching skills to Iowa, and waited to hear about the teaching assistantship.

Around seven of a Friday morning in late March I was sitting on a plastic and aluminum chaise longue on the apartment's tiny balcony, bundled in blankets, sipping coffee and trying to read Sophocles in the meager light of false dawn, waiting for the sun to come up.

I yawned, bored, tried to dig back into the *Electra*... and knew, could sense on the first ring of the phone, that some dreadful other shoe had fallen somewhere.

"Miller?..Miller boy, that you? That you there?"

It was Sonney Macready: sweet and frail, old since I'd known him as a boy, white-haired, liver-spotted...he would be in his 80s, I calculated. "Yeah...yeah, it's me, Sonney, what's cooking?"

"Miller, I got some...bad news for you..." I could see his watery blue eyes, his liver-blotched hands on the earpiece of the phone in the booth at Elgin's Sinclair station, where he'd probably driven to make the call; he hated to use the telephone. Girded as I thought I was, I wasn't nor could ever have got ready

118

for his next words: "Miller, your pa...he's gone and up and died on us."

Out of nowhere I recalled Malcolm X's words about Kennedy's assassination that had caused such a furor: *All the chickens have come home to roost.* Except for one.

I could see Sonney partly supporting himself on a bent elbow resting on the metal ledge under the pay phone.

"What happened?"

"They was a fire to your place last night."

"Fire? What happened, Sonney?"

"Wellsir, they say he died from inhaling smoke and it wouldn't've hurt him none, don't you see, he was working late in the shop, it's the shop was burned down to almost nothing..."

"Down to nothing? You mean they can't find nothing of him in the shop?" I began instantly constructing an alternative: Turner had fabricated a ruse, decided to light out for the Caribbean—one of my own fantasies—or to secrete himself in the far reaches of the Upper Penninsula he knew so well, he had rigged it all so I'd get the insurance and he'd disappear. Hell, he was only just over fifty and strong and healthy as a horse...so maybe...

But then Sonney got enough spit in his craw to scotch that: "His legs was there," Sonney said.

My own throat went dry as a leaf in winter, but I moved my jaws and some words came out: "I'll be coming home, Sonney."

The air seemed to buzz. I felt numb as I walked to the kitchen and took my unopened pint of Jim Beam from the shelf. I went into the living-dining room and set it on the coffee table and sat in the easy chair that came with the place; but then before I could even break the seal on the bottle it came boiling out of me, laughter, laughter, I rolled back in the chair and howled and jerked and barked, grotesque yawps a banshee could've been proud of.

*

That was morning. Around noon I passed through Cadillac in the VW, leaving at last behind me the flat fulsome landscape of south-central Michigan and moving into the north.

I had a short belt of Beam to bevel down the edges of my nerves.

119

I thought of all the cerebral hate I lavished on Bernard Dunstable whom I still held responsible for Rex's death, though I was by now willing to concede that maybe Rex and I hadn't been too smart either—especially me: for that had been me that night, hadn't it, filled with a mixture of pride and exultancy from having—this was how I felt it then—*won*, for by having outfoxed the college pricks and got my two sheepskins that Turner set such store by, I'd shown the bastards what a swamp-rat with a good brain could do. And though I could still yearn to seek out Burner in some secret place and drive my hard right fist like a jackhammer into his windpipe over and over until it was good and broken, I knew too that under different circumstances Burner and I could probably've bellied up to a barn and laid out, each for the other's inspection, our respective and corresponding hatreds for the ski trash, resorters, maybe even life in general.

I tromped hard on the gas pedal and the little VW shuddered as it reached seventy-five and we hurtled on through leaden skies toward home.

SEVEN

Instead of dressing Lindsay said to hell with it, put her robe on over her underwear and with a sour expression brushed out her hair in the bathroom.

Glaring at her image, she thought she could discern a series of lines like miniature lacerations around her eyes, no doubt the spidery signature of recent strain; but it was surely only temporary—she was way too young to have real wrinkles. Even rather beat like this she had to admit she was still quite pretty. In fact, Miller'd always been most aroused by her when she was a bit disheveled—she'd never known whether to feel chagrin or pride at the fact.

She opened her bedroom door. Down the hall the door to the master bedroom was ajar and she heard her mother's TV going: "Missuss Goodman, you have won twennywunhunnerd dollars! I don't be-*lieve* it!" screamed a male emcee and shrill cries of hysterical cupidity keened about him.

She crept stealthily past and down the stairs.

The kitchen blazed and the flourescent lights gave everything white a stark look, as if the place were being readied for surgery.

"Hi, honey."

"Hi, Daddy." Her father sat at the round breakfast table before French doors opening onto a brick patio, glumly sipping a cup of something. He loosed a slack, fluttering sigh, which he terminated with a click of his tongue.

"Whatcha drinking?"

"Peppermint tea."

"Mmmm..." Through the French doors she could see the pool Vernon Noel had had built in 1957, its emptiness accentuated by a trio of spotlights at its base. "Mom wrote you were doing something with the pool?"

"Yeah...I was going to have it heated, then decided not to. Ran out of steam. Had visions of myself bounding out of bed at

121

six and doing some laps...but hell, why lie. I only got so much energy any more, I haven't even filled it since I had it drained for an estimate on the heating apparatus. Sorry it's not filled for you." He brightened a little. "I'll get cracking on it soon's I get the guy out here to fix the filter..."

"No, no, don't, not on my account...I meant to tell you in the car on the way home, you know, the way you look—"

"—yeah, yeah, yeah: like an old fart who's trimmed off a little lard, yeah, I know what I am but thanks, thanks anyway..."

"No, I mean it, but seriously—"

"Yeah, I know. But I'm still middle-aged, no matter how you cut it. I started thirty years too late. But for whatever reason, I laid off the sauce...starting taking vitamins, watching my cholesterol and all that...now I take vitamin C, E, zinc, lecithin, various things...dessicated liver, brewer's yeast—stuff like that."

"Goodness." She felt like giggling.

"Not to mention, as you may not have noticed, I'm also off cigars...sugar, salt, Christ. Guess I'm just trying like everybody else to prolong the sweet agony of living. Bertha's kicking the bucket I guess put the fear of God into me or something."

"Goodness. How's Mom taking all this?"

"Oh, well, you know...Wyn. I mean after Bertha she for a time got to depend on Screwdrivers at lunch, and then she'd switch from her novel to TV in the afternoons and start on Scotch until it got so she was putting it away pretty steadily, almost to the point it was a danger, you know, dry teapot left on over the flame, burning cigarettes here and there...but, bless her heart, when I went on my regime—or regimen or whatever the hell it's supposed to be—she slowed down of her own account. Doesn't touch the sauce until evening, or hardly ever before, and, you know, keeps the edges planed down with Librium and an occasional phenobarb, and of course there's the grand climacteric—hey! I thought we were supposed to work out *your* problems, not hash over our more-or-less solved ones..."

Lindsay peered out through the French doors again: the moon was rising like a luminous globe of some ripe fruit, heavy and full. She thought of Miller and his fascination with moons—once in Iowa City when they were coiled together in an after-coital drowse, she'd murmured something about the moonlight falling through the window and Miller'd murmured back, half-

122

conscious, "Wonder why a full moon gives me a hard-on?"—and wondered what he was doing at this precise moment. ("Don't blame your imperfections on the moon," she'd murmured back, biting his shoulder lightly, but he was falling asleep again.)

"On the way over from Traverse," her father began, "did I not infer that maybe you're *not* done with Miller, as you'd sounded when you called from O'Hare?" This was his "talk turkey" voice, neither harsh nor peremptory, but nonetheless probing: "So let's take it from the top, shall we, sweetheart, and play it by ear and all that: so tell me, what seems to be the trouble?"

She wasn't ready for this, at least not yet; she evaded: "You tell me, Doctor. God, I'm tired. Can you get jet lag just coming from Iowa? Probably a good night's sleep'll clear a lot of things up, huh?" (For this was after all his line for all those years, and he really believed it.)

"Yeah...well, to really put you out, want me to stir you up my famous Noel sleeping potion? You're so tense, maybe we ought to put off, uh, substantive things until tomorrow..."

"Thanks, Daddy, but absolutely: I'm all in, I'm not up to much right now, but I *am* tense..."

Vernon Noel hoisted himself up from his chair and plucked a huge pill bottle from the counter, shook a large beige pill into his hand, and popped it into his mouth like an after-dinner mint: "Vitamin C from rosehips and acerola, chewable, 500 migs, good for the nerves," he said, chewing sturdily. "Want one?"

"No thanks. But it's me, mostly...and him too...and even things I'd never considered would be important in my life...like money..."

"Money! When we're practically rolling in it, hell, the Skeegemog Agency makes as much as I ever did in Bay City..."

"But Daddy: once we got settled and Miller was in school and all, what do you think we lived on? *Love?* We had to hand-to-mouth it, as Miller says, I mean we had to live on his Teaching Assistant money and my waitressing money. I mean we didn't have any mortgage to pay on, but we had taxes and water and gas and electricity and food and tuition and when we had to buy a new refrigerator from Sears it was three hundred dollars! It was over a hundred dollars for snow tires for the Volvo...and there was car and house insurance. I mean I know I took along my three thousand in savings, but my God, I mean we had to have some furniture and things, and I needed decent *things*, Daddy! God, Miller'd've got everything from the Goodwill or something, he *likes* old used things, but the only thing that made Iowa bearable was to have some nice things, like the furniture and rugs and *things* I got!"

"Christ, Lindsay! Why wouldn't you let me give you some money—or lend it to you if you or Miller insisted. I mean, like I *told* you, anything, anytime, you can always count on me, we're *family*, damnit, and there's something just plain wrong if not downright sinful for you two kids to squat out there in the middle of nowhere, I mean I applaud self-reliance and all that, hell, that's what's made our country the greatest in history, but on the other hand this foolish pride..." He hunched forward until his knee nearly touched her knee. He was wearing the same shaving lotion Randy Wilder used, Marcel Rochas' "Moustache"—or something awfully close. "You know, I guess I have gathered together a good deal of what people mean when they say The Finer Things in Life, and I want you to know I'm happy I've got someone to pass it on to someday. And I presume you'll have sons and daughters someday to pass on what I've passed on to you, and that's the idea of things, but...but tell you what, you need to get a good night's sleep, and so now without further ado I'll just whip up my stupefyingly effective nightcap, guaranteed better than phenobarb. Okay?"

She followed him in to the wet bar in the living room.

"All righty," she said, seeking a cheerful note, "but surely you don't mean one of those champagne cocktails of yours, do you? You mean the tequila gimlet with a Scotch float, right?"

"The very same! You haven't forgotten."

"Then I'll have one. But Daddy, doesn't it bother you to have other people drinking around you when you're not?" Then she noticed he was building two drinks.

"Not until just now," he said cheerfully, pouring tequila into a double-ended shot measure, his wrist-flick deft as any bartender's.

"Daddy," she began doubtfully.

He came jauntily around the bar, holding the two glasses aloft as though thus yoked they constituted some unwieldy chalice. "Not to worry," he said easily, "I never swore off the sauce formally, I only did it because of the calories and because

124

alcohol washes out and neutralizes the salutary aspects of the vitamins. You ever read *Prevention* magazine? Well, you ought to. But what the hell, I owe myself a little something. I deserve it. I'm entitled. Cheers."

"Cheers."

EIGHT

Driving from Mt. Haven toward whatever I was to find in Ermine Falls, where now my father, save for what remained of his legs, was no more, I could not avoid reviewing still again that March morning a week after Rex's death when I left for Mt. Haven and my inconsequential—except as a device for increasing my chances to a teaching assistantship at Iowa—job at the university's writing lab: the morning of my defection, desertion, whatever you want to call it. As I drove I found myself so filled with guilt and self-loathing (or maybe self-pity, it's all pretty much the same thing) I would not have have bridled at some third party's judgment, no matter how severe it might be: indeed I might have welcomed it.

*

When we sit briefly at the kitchen table with coffee after I have loaded my VW with books and odds and ends, some of which I'd brought home a few weeks earlier, I think I catch a glimpse of uncharacteristic slyness or evasion curling around the dead-ashes emptiness that comes and goes in Turner's eyes these bleak days.

"Reckon come spring you'll set that west cornfield to pine seedlings like you figured you might?" I am compelled to insist there will be a future though I fear in my heart it is already leaving like some implacable train sliding away from a dreary station in the middle of nowhere. I think of Chekhov en route to Sakhalin Island and the horrors he will find there.

"No. I don't have much planting left in me."

"What'll you do with it, then?"

"Have it seeded for pasture, maybe."

"What for?" Our last cow had died in the fall and Turner'd used the backhoe to bury her on our property up near the old orchard, and he hadn't got another; now, with Rex gone and me

126

leaving, there couldn't have seemed much need for one except maybe as a pet, something you could listen to as it tore mouthfuls of damp grass from the pasture.

He turns to me and speaks with a sudden though quiet intensity: "Listen, Miller, want you to know that if anything was ever to happen to me, well, then, there's papers in my bureau drawer—insurance and deeds and bank books and things...so if anything ever happens that you need to dig'em out, you just do it, and if it should happen I'm ever gone, then you just sell the whole fucking works, lock, stock and barrel and get the hell out and don't look back, go live in some college town, maybe that one in Iowa you're thinking about going to, that's where you should be, at some big good school taking your rightful place with them other brainy word-workers."

"I reckon I got a good many hard years before I get anywhere in the professor business...I ain't even sure I can take two-three years of Iowa, don't know as I much like that flat country—all hogs and cornfields, you ought to see the way the sun flashes off them corrugated metal things they got for the hogs so's they don't get sunburnt...but let's us not worry about way in the future like that, what're you'n me going to do otherwise, now, I mean, in the meantime...?"

"Meantime?" He snorts mirthlessly. "What the hell's that? You learnt to college what the meantime is, eh? I'd ask you to teach me, but I'm the old dog in the proverb, as I reckon I've shown pretty good by now: I ain't any good for new tricks no more. Don't know as I'd recognize Mister Meantime if he up and bit me in the ass."

*

I rounded the last corner in the VW, and when I first saw the blackened rubble and caved-in walls of the shop, my heart lurched in my chest like some stricken animal, my guts turned to water and my mouth went dry as a stone.

I kept my eyes off it and pulled into the drive as if I were normally coming home for a weekend; and I kept them off it as I went to the front door and turned the knob.

It was unlocked. I went in.

It was just as if I'd come home under normal circumstances:

127

a cup and saucer sat on the dining room table, there was a newspaper protecting the tabletop from a shiny transmission spline and two sets of ball bearings...and yet it was empty, too, and not silent in its emptiness, for there was a kind of spectral ringing in the air: or was it only in my mind—

That was it!

*

My face was on the carpet: I'd rolled off the Hideabed in the study in Iowa City and onto the floor. Just under the Hideabed I could see a sheepskin lined slipper Lindsay'd been looking for for weeks.

Then I remembered why the dream'd probably thrown me from the sofa: because of how our dead house in Ermine Falls rang, a bit like Lindsay insisted this place rang when we came here, before there was a stick of furniture in it: it was spooky, she said, but seemed inclined to think back then that the ringing was benevolent, because according to her a-ring with hope and future and a chance to cut the cloth of life properly if we just had the wherewithal, which she was convinced we did—

But the house in Ermine Falls: it had suddenly become a husk whose spirit had fled or been chased away, perhaps by the desecration it had been witness to, which I suspected now negated every pleasant thing that had ever happened within its walls.

I walked into our kitchen in Ermine Falls and there, sitting on the table, were six square frosted-glass bottles of Gilbey's gin, lined up neatly. One was full, with the seal unbroken; the others were empty.

Then I laughed: and by God then the house *rang*: rocked and echoed with my howling laughter I had loosed for the second time that day, and I lurched out into the living room and had to clutch Turner's easy chair for support as tears streamed from my eyes.

Perhaps there was some catharsis in it all, because as my spasms of black mirth that were getting dangerously close to weeping began to subside, I felt a sudden warmth as though I'd just drunk some whiskey: I thought I could feel Turner's strong arm around my shoulders, then there was the suggestion of a voice in my inner ear softly saying a single word: *Pal*, it seemed

128

to say. *Pal.* That was all and I never heard it again.

I wheeled into the kitchen and took a long drink from the full bottle of Gilbey's, then went out the door to drive down and see the Macready's.

*

It had begun to darken outside now, but I didn't have the wherewithal to check the time. I wondered for the thousandth time where Lindsay was, what doing, whether or not I'd ever see her again, whether we might ever live together again and—yes, God help me—if I'd ever fuck her again; the briefest suggestion of that was all it took for me to spring a hard-on and I decided it was time to switch from beer back to Jim Beam. Like Turner in those days before his death, I had been forethinking enough to lay in a reasonable supply— which was to say, more than I could reasonably drink.

NINE

It was 11:30. Her father'd drained his drink an hour earlier in several swift gulps—and soon after he'd arisen as if on a string, belched, excused himself, thumped his chest with his fist, winced, cleared his throat and said: "Jesus, I all of a sudden don't feel so hot, kiddo...maybe I overdid it a bit with the big schooner of sauce...maybe I'll just hit the hay and like we said we'll go into everything tomorrow..."

She was in the den on the leather sofa. Johnny Carson was on the TV, but she kept the sound off and sipped at the third of the Bloody Marys she'd made after Vernon'd made his exit—she'd been able to manage no more than a few sips of the drink he'd made her, which turned out to taste like ground cork or something, though she thought she'd once been fond of it.

She felt so fatigued she could hardly move, yet her enervation contained no pleasant lassitude: how can you be sleepy and antsy at the same time? she wondered.

As she drowsed with the flickering TV providing the only light, she thought about poor dead Rex Springstead, and wondered how much what he had done for her years ago had to do with how easily she'd either seduced or let herself be seduced by his brother Miller something over a year ago. And why had she never told Miller—or anyone else, for that matter?

Rex'd led her to the door of the second floor fire escape as she'd begged so that she might go down the outside metal steps covered with a kind of galvanized metal tunnel which would leave her in the teacher's parking lot. Before she entered the dark tunnel she turned to him and whispered, "If it weren't for you I'd've just *died*..." He pressed her hand once with his strong fingers, winked, and was gone. She never saw him again.

She walked the mile and a half home, once ducking out of sight behind a tree when she saw a school bus.

I must have been a pretty little picture with my cardigan tied around my hips as I stomped all the way home, because after the

130

fear of Basil ebbed I felt rage and not rage at Basil but at Daddy and Ermine Falls because they'd *let* it happen, I was so mad and determined I could spit nails, I was never *ever* going to set foot inside Ermine Falls School no matter what, they'd have to kill me first. And when I got home Daddy was already there and Mom was out having her hair done. I must have looked frightful because Daddy put aside his afternoon bowl of corn flakes and blueberries and trotted over to me wearing that white-lipped look he had when I'd fallen out of one of the Chinese elms in the backyard in Bay City when I was nine or so and knocked the wind out of myself and could only moan and gasp. I slipped past him and ran upstairs, staring to cry again and took care of myself in the bathroom while he waited anxiously outside, every now and then calling in, "Lindsay? Lindsay? Sweetheart, are you all right? Answer me, please!" "Yes, *yes*," I'd say back, "yes, let me *alone*, go downstairs, I'll be out in a few minutes..."

So finally later on when we were in the den, he had a drink and he gave me a little glass with some brandy that tasted of orange peel and made me feel a little better and almost grown-up enough to tell him what'd happened, but all I could say to him was, "I'm not going back to school, not to that school ever, Daddy! And I don't care and isn't it just too bad but I won't!" He kept trying in the nicest way to find out *exactly what happened*— "Lindsay, baby, now, it's all going to be okay, but first we've got to *know*, don't you see?" But no, I couldn't see, so when he persisted I just blurted out the first stuff that came into my head (which wasn't necessarily untrue, either): "Oh, Daddy, it's just that...just that they all stink! Daddy! All of them. Except for Evonne they're *all* alike, just stupid and mean and I hate that cheerleader stuff, the teachers are dumb, I speak better English than they do, in the ninth grade here we have spelling exercises like I had in the sixth grade in Bay City. I can't learn anything here! I want to go to a good school! I won't go back! I hate this part of the state!"

"Well, Lord, honey, I realize it's hardly Country Day in Grosse Point or Bloomfield Hills, but...there must be something more to this...maybe I could get you into Skeegemog..."

"Well, there isn't any more to anything! And I don't want to go here any more and I won't go back! And I'm *not* going to go to Skeegemog or any other awful little hick town either!"

131

Lindsay was in her room an hour later when Vernon came to tell her to come downstairs.

Wyn Noel's eyes were wet and red around the edges but they were hard and bright at the centers. In spite of having her hair done, a few wispy ends were loose and her cheeks were flushed and Lindsay could smell on her the same brandy she herself had drunk earlier. She started before Lindsay sat down: "So here you are and you get this wonderful chance to be a big fish in a small pond, by which I mean being a cheerleader and acting in plays and making your own little contribution to things and making your parents proud of you and you're just too good for it all!" Her outrage plucked her from the chair and she faced Lindsay angrily, hands balled on her hips. They were almost the same height. "Now see what you've done, little Miss Too Good For It All? You know, Lindsay"—she paled suddenly and looked genuinely ill— "I think you've made me sick. Oh yes, I'm a little sick and I have to go to the bathroom..." She swept past her daughter and in moment she and her father could hear her flushing the upstairs john.

By the time Wyn flushed it a second time, Vernon was already on the phone to his sister, Lindsay's Aunt Roxanne, in Ann Arbor: "Uh-huh...I'm glad to hear that, and we'll of course be counting on you for Thanksgiving...but say, I'm glad I was finally able to reach you, Rox, there's a reason for this call beyond...oh, whatever the hell it is. Anyway, you know all those invitations you're always extending to your favorite niece? Are they still on? Uh-huh? Great. Listen, you're always telling me what a hotshot place University High is, and how Lindsay ought to go to someplace like that? Well..."

Mom never did come back and later when I went upstairs, I tiptoed on the thick carpet past her room. I could hear the TV on low, and just as I passed I heard her snort in derision and mutter something. Then I heard ice cubes in a pitcher and I realized that at some point while Daddy and I had been talking she'd slipped down the stairs—fumbling for drinks when she might've pressed me to her and patted my shoulder and hugged me and told me over and over, It's all right, it's all right, it's all right.

*

Lindsay awoke on the leather sofa. The TV was off and there was a blanket over her—Vernon obviously had come down to check on her and decided to let her sleep on.

Certainly her mother wouldn't have covered her up and tucked in the edges like this. Only Daddy'd have taken the time and care to do it this nicely.

TEN

At about eight in the evening two days after Turner's death I stood on the deep carpeting of the O'Donnell Funeral Home in Skeegemog wearing my old sport coat and suit pants—Rex'd been buried in my suit coat, so it was all I had. The carpeting felt like it was rising around my ankles like quicksand.

After I'd polished off Turner's remaining fifth of gin at home, I'd bought six more bottles, Gilbey's of course, and they had thus far helped keep me sufficently anesthetized to get through things. Except at the moment I felt stone sober. I yearned to go out to the VW for a nip, but Sonney and Pearl were there on either side of me and it wouldn't have been seemly.

I felt a surge of love for both of them—in a way they'd been more our parents than Turner had, and had raised me and Rex as their own during the war years. Pearl was wispier now, more stooped, while Sonney too was aging perceptibly. They'd seemed aged to me even back when they were taking care of us while Turner was at the war, but I'd thought them somehow ageless beyond what they were, impervious to time, but now in my 20s I could see they were just like everybody else and I could only pray when their ends came they would do so almost simultaneously—it was heartbreaking to think of either going on without the other.

We stood before Turner's polished wood coffin, the one I'd picked out, and I wondered morbidly what was really in it: was there really a set of heat-and-smoke wizened legs in there, a welter of charred flesh, protruding bone, crumbling tendons and ligaments? Were they intact enough to appear as giant cooked frog's legs? I felt a compulsion to run to the coffin, wrench the lid off, and dump whatever might be inside onto the bottomless-feeling claret-colored carpeting and scream, "See! See! Goddamnit! Do you all see?"

Religious music was piped through various hidden speakers, bland and cloying. Tomorrow whatever was in the coffin would be buried in the Clearwater Township Cemetary next to Rex.

Small snow and a reasonable temperatures at least meant neither Rex nor Turner had to wait in refrigeration for the spring thaw. Turner'd bought four plots there some years back, so there was plenty of room for me there, too. Maybe I should get cracking on my own tombstone while I'm at it, I thought giddily. Let's see:

Miller M. Springstead
1940-19

No, what the hell, gamble on it; put down: 1940-196 and then whoever scrapes up whatever's left of me after I've hit whatever Christawful stump I'm destined to hit when the last shoe falls'll have but a single digit to chisel into the granite. Hell, maybe I'll go the whole route:

Miller M. Springstead, B.A., M.A.
1940-1967
"Vulnerability didn't make him humble",

which'll maybe ultimately be the best that can be said of me. Sorry, Turner. Pal. Unless of course I actually do perservere these next few years and get my PhD, then I could add that to my summation. But at the moment I regarded that exalted degree like it was Everest or K-2, some monolith so dwarfing my abilities that my only refuge lay in insignificance, obscurity and gin.

*

It was in another room in this same funeral home where a little less than a month earlier Turner and I had stood before Rex's gunmetal coffin (chosen by Turner). I shut my eyes, a puff of gin rose dangerously in my throat. Though Rex's coffin was to be kept closed, O'Donnell, popularly called "Digger," seemed a bit disappointed by that fact, and nearly insisted that we view what he called the "remains": "I want you to see the work was done," he said, lifting the part that covered the top half of the corpse, and therein languished a kind of effigy of Rex in my suit coat. The color of its cheeks was high, they were slightly pink in the centers, like Turner's in the winter, and its faint expression, intended to convey a cheerful, gentle sleep, was somewhere between a smirk and a half-grin. I could feel a corresponding grimace begin to twist at my jawbones and heard Rex whisper in my inner ear, *Je-suss, ain't this kick in the slats, Miller, here they fucking drain you and dude you up with lipstick and rouge and shit like that like you're off to the queers' convention, sorry to've took your suit coat...*

I'd looked at Turner, standing there next to me, slowly twisting and turning his black wool watch cap in his hands as though it was rosary beads, and realized that this scene to which he had finally been brought, to stand here before the coffin of his eldest boy, the one in some ways closer to him than his younger one, was the worst thing that could have befallen him, its bleakness perhaps beyond the horrors of death and carnage lived and witnessed when he was a Marine in the South Pacific, worse even than the horrible day he got me out of jail the morning after Rex's death by gunshot—at least the shock and movement called for would have given him small refuge. Here there was none.

Though we were so close our shoulders might brush I knew there was nothing I—or anyone else—could do or say, for I sensed some final partitioning of Turner's soul had already taken place and he was now virtually beyond the pale of anyone's thought or deed.

As always, I had—a defense mechanism I reckon the shrinks would say—a handy literary quote to repeat to myself; appropriately enough I'd been re-reading the Oedipus dramas of Sophocles, and I recalled the Chorus' words to the audience at Colonus: "Not to be born surpasses thought and speech. The second best is to have seen the light/ And then to go back quickly whence we came."

Turner continued to stand there beside me, statue-like, only his hands working in his cap, our shoulders almost touching, as we looked upon Rex.

Then O'Donnell closed the lid and Rex disappeared forever.

Yes, I thought, yes, yes, not being born is truly beyond all prizing.

*

And here I stood again, before another coffin, fearful that I might laugh at the horror and absurdity of it all, even with Pearl and Sonney on either side, and I thought again: Yes, surely, not being born is beyond all prizing.

Sonney squeezed my one arm and Pearl pressed closer, taking the other. "Come on now, Miller, steady, boy, you been a fur piece today, we been here long enough, now, and you come along home with us."

"I reckon," I said, my eyes on the glossy wood of the closed coffin before me, "I reckon."

*

Over the next few days, I cleaned the house, furiously, obsessively, on my hands and knees with rags and Spic'n Span and brushes. I did the walls, grubbed each last stain from the porcelain in the bathroom like some demented charwoman who couldn't stop cleaning, working on compulsively until the gin I fueled myself coupled with my fatigue to the point where I had to collapse on the living room sofa and sleep for a few hours.

I got rid of almost everything I wasn't giving away to Sonney and Pearl. The appliances and some of the furniture I was keeping, so I stored them in the barn, thinking I might take some of the stuff to Iowa if I followed through and actually went there. It was all relatively easy because Turner wasn't a packrat, hadn't kept old papers, letters, bills, and except for records for income tax purposes he was always big on throwing away anything he wouldn't likely need.

Right after Rex's death Turner had had a lawyer draw up a quit-claim deed so that in the event of his death all the real estate and other property of his was also in my name and there was no need for inheritance taxes or even dealing with the Probate Court in Skeegemog; and he made out a brief will, too, just in case the Probate Court got involved, which I tucked away. After the legal phrasing it contained a single sentence: "All my property, real and personal, I leave to my only surviving son, Miller M. Springstead."

Some things of Turner's I kept for myself: his Jap sword, his old 9mm pistol, a set of socket wrenches that hadn't gone up in the shop, his winter cap, his steel thermos we'd once got him for Christmas, and some other odds and ends.

As I was taking care of these things, keeping myself just

137

sober enough so as not to screw anything up, a letter forwarded to Ermine Falls from Mt. Haven came for me from the University of Iowa: I'd gotten the teaching assistantship.

And so as Turner had wanted me to do, I would leave, go, turn my back on where I grew up and try to start a life up elsewhere—or at least find out if it was possible. Things were for me such a muddle it was hard to know if any sort of order or peace would ever be possible.

The last thing I got rid of was Turner's beloved Hallicrafter's Sky Buddy. I couldn't bear to keep it myself though something in me wanted to, but I knew that everytime I turned it on I'd feel as though somebody'd jabbed a pitchfork tine into my heart. So I took it down to Sonney and Pearl's the evening before I went back to Mt. Haven. They were there—I could see light behind the pulled blinds—but I couldn't bear to see them and it together so I slipped up noiselessly and left it on the back porch where Rex and I had played so many hours those war years while Turner was away. I couldn't stand any more talk or goodbyes just now.

I went back to our place and sat in the dark in Turner's leather easy chair by the dining room window which the Macreadys would come and get after I was gone. I would never be able to bear its presence in Iowa.

It was comfortable as ever. But my task wasn't. I sat there with a bottle of gin in my hand from which I occasionally drank and completed my last task of leave-taking: I had to re-live Turner's end.

I ran my fingers over the scuff marks in the back of the chair where the cross-piece of his suspenders had roughened the leather over the years. Here he'd sat as Rex and I grew up and went to school and then Rex to the Army and a little later me to college, drinking coffee, listening to the news over the Sky Buddy.

And now it is the final evening of his life.

I feel myself merging with him as he rises for the last time from the chair's comfortable depths in his characteristic fashion, his powerful arms thrusting as they alone raise him on legs now a bit shaky from gin, the taste of which is brackish in his mouth, his stomach is curdled, his breath sour—probably he'd aged years in the short time he'd been back on the sauce. He'd taken pleasure in his strength of limb over the years, but this time he'd see it as a curse, something that had for a time given him the illusion of another kind of strength.

The Sky Buddy is silent, hasn't been on in days.

He sinks back just once onto the cushion, hesitates for a few seconds as he thinks of his boys, then gets up from it for the last time. He guzzles from the quarter full bottle of gin, draining it.

He gets another full bottle, cracks the seal, has a short drink, wobbles into the bathroom, takes a piss, then goes out the door and makes his way to the shop.

Once inside, he sits heavily on the metal chair by the table on which sit his oversized adding machine and volumes of parts manuals; it's where he toted up receipts for years and where he used to do his income taxes.

He takes another drink, then turns to his chest of Snap-On tools and fits a socket onto an extension, then snaps the extension onto a ratchet wrench. He takes another drink.

Then, slowly, so he doesn't risk puking, he drinks all the rest of the fifth of gin. So drunk he can barely navigate, he spills one of the many kinds of flammable fluids you can find in the shop on the cement floor and onto some nearby exposed wall joists— and then probably sets a small candle that'll burn down and ignite it in fifteen minutes or so in the middle of the puddle. Turner even drunk was no suburban fool blowing himself up at his charcoal grill with lighter fluid: he'd have known exactly what he was doing.

Then he takes his ratchet wrench, crawls onto the creeper and scoots himself under the pickup and shuts his eyes and passes out—this last stroke so he won't look like the suicide he is.

Before the gin extinguishes his mind I hope he has one moment of peace: I hope he hears the sound our cow used to make tearing at the damp green grass near the spring in the pasture; or feels himself sitting once again by the screened window in the living room on a summer evening, the Sky Buddy silent of the horrors of the world, while he pins his attention on the barn swallows disporting themselves at dusk and then, a little later, the moonlit night pierced by a whip-poor-will's cry, and I hope he thinks of his boys slumbering upstairs with nothing more complex than school and baseball and pussy on their minds and feels restful enough to sleep.

139

*

I waken on the Hideabed in the study in Iowa City at three in the morning—"in the true dark night of the soul it is always three in the morning, night after night," right?—feeling neither drunk nor sober. I recognize this particular rung on the ladder of disintegration: where you look pretty much okay but are shaky, where the horrible can seem funny, the mundane terrifying, and where you can mount to a sodden rapture in the blink of an eye or plunge equally rapidly to despair, where virtually all things you encounter seem to be symbols crouching behind masks no matter how literally corporeal they may be. And of course the only cure, or rather the anodyne that'll permit you to momentarily hold at bay whatever's due to come crashing down, is some more sauce: here it's coin of the realm and you use it to buy you a little time in a corner away from it all where you can maybe figure out where the fuck and what the fuck.

Yes, a drink, but no hard stuff, Miller, ole hoss: no hard stuff, just some brew to bevel the rough edges down a tad—

I get up, thinking of the Clearwater Cemetary in Ermine Falls where both Rex and Turner are buried. To get there you drive out south of town and turn off on Cemetary Road and drive for, say, a quarter of a mile before the cemetary comes into view. It lies in two portions on either side of the meandering dirt road which bisects it and then winds upward through the hills where Rex and I used to hike and hunt.

To the left is the larger and older part, dating back to the 1840s, where maybe 300 people lie. There's a chapel there, a well-built clapboard structure that was once a one-room country school, moved here and modified by the WPA.

To the right lies the smaller and less well-kept portion, about seven acres, say, and at its outermost perimeters the land starts to rise upward. Just where the land begins to lift, the cemetary is abruptly reclaimed by young woods and bracken where all is wild and disordered: ferns, sumac, thistles, vetch, berry bushes...then comes the denser covering of trees, mostly maple, hemlock and poplar, which seem not so much to lean as to march upward, and as the hill continues to steepen, the trees crowd closer and closer together until like frozen mountain climbers trapped in ascent, they strain, motionless but alive, toward the summit.

140

It is there where the cemetary begins to turn into hill that Rex and Turner lie.

*

In the kitchen I pop a cold beer and drink it slowly as I make two soft boiled eggs. But when I break them into a coffee cup, one has a blood spot and I barely make it into the bathroom before I am engulfed by a pulsing series of gut-wrenching convulsions that bring up the beer and a little bile and I am left gasping on the floor, clinging to the cool porcelain stool. And yet as the spasms ebb, I begin to feel light-headed and pretty good, though flaccid as after making love...which must be one of the few moments of absolute peace on earth, at least after you get over that split-second of fear just after your orgasm, something built in to the species, I suppose, because you're so totally vulnerable to your enemies when getting laid.

I wash my face off with a sopping cold wash rag and confront myself in the mirror: *Ecce homo*: not too bad, I look as though a shower and shave might almost bring me back to normal. But underneath I know, don't I, that nothing in this world will—can—ever really do that.

Turner once told me the best way to quit drinking was, you imagined yourself having the first few and very best drinks of a bender, when you felt loose and witty and at peace with the things that had just been nagging you...and then you visualized in total detail the steps that followed: the on-creeping sense of befuddlement, yourself becoming any of a number of ways, stupid, aggressive, violent, bitter, or filled with moronic hilarity...you continue on carefully, imagining your progress until the moment you wake the next morning and take that first utterly shattering look at the light of day and the bitter knowledge that hair of the dog that bit you is the only thing'll cure you. If you did that carefully, Turner thought, that might stay your hand from the sauce. If you were basically a good enough of a man to begin with, that is.

I spy a glass of Jim Beam on the top of the toilet tank, still half full: Come to me, my little firefly. Down the hatch.

ELEVEN

Lindsay was up early and on the road by eight. A thin brume hovered over the black tape of Highway 31 and the tops of telephone poles and trees were still nimbused with diaphanous swirls of dissolving fog. ("Evanescent," she remembered Miller saying not all that long ago: "Evanescent, evanescent, I love that word, Conrad uses it all the time. Everything is evanescent, thank Christ for that, huh? Wouldn't existence itself be shit on a stick if it weren't endowed like everything else with evanescence, I mean relatively speaking? Can't say I'm crazy about Swinburne in general, but aren't these lines kinda neat: 'From too much love of living, From hope and fear set free, Let us thank with brief thanksgiving, Whatever gods may be, That no man lives forever, That dead men rise up never, That even the loneliest river, Winds somewhere safe to sea'—think that's from 'In the Garden of Proserpine'...which further reminds me, Conrad said somewhere that you could tell every man's biography in eight words, 'He was born, he suffered and he died'..Conrad reminds me of Faulkner, who admired that line and who wrote somewhere, 'Between grief and nothing, I'll take grief'...everything seems to remind me of something else...I think it's in *Sartor Resartus* that the guy says, 'Happiness is stupidity and a sound digestion'...")

Probably it would turn into a gorgeous daffodil and carnation of a day as soon as the sun torched away the haze and turned the road to platinum and the sky to cheery azure.

She drove her mother's compact robin's-egg blue Cutlass convertible. She felt pretty good, all things considered. She'd been hungry, had eaten a good breakfast, and had kept a pleasant look pasted on her face as Wyn offered some palliative small talk: "...not so much these late summer mornings but the ones in early fall are the ones I love best for sleeping, I don't know why but fall is my favorite season..."

"In Iowa it's not so much the heat as the humidity," Lindsay had offered.

"I suppose. Oh, and *do* remember, dear, Mr. Dalyrimple—

you know, the minister of whom I spoke to you of last night? Well, just a reminder that he'll be here for lunch and afterward we'll all be sure to leave you and he alone and I want you to talk to him and be utterly frank with him about your...domestic situation. I've heard wonderful things of him and he's such a pleasant young man for someone so young. Hilary will serve promptly at one, and I know she'll want to fix something special because we decided to let you sleep straight through last night, you were so exhausted..."

*

She drove on. Mist dissipated into ragged scraps and, as the sun began to shine with a hard brilliance, heat rose in shimmery waves above the road. Lindsay clipped along at fifty, toward Silverfish Lake eight miles away, where Evonne now lived.

It was intriguing that Evonne had married a local—when they'd both worked at the Hills during the past three summers, Evonne had seemed spiteful to locals: "C'mon, c'mon," she'd shrill at some adolescent breaking in as a busboy, "Clean the potatoes out of your ears, there, Pud, and hop it!" Or to that poor kid Floyd Gruber, who'd got demoted from busboy to potwasher summer before last because Milton thought he looked like somebody'd used a bowl when they gave him a haircut (which was entirely possible): "Come *on*, get a wiggle on, Lard, let's see you hustle butt!"

God knows plenty of out-of-staters were hot for her: Evonne often wore huge blonde Dutch-girl braids, and she had a delicately formed brow, nose and cheekbones, while her generous mouth was a sunburst bristling with handsome symmetrical teeth, and you couldn't be sure if she was just attractive or truly beautiful (the former from the side, the latter from the front, Lindsay had decided).

And when she'd told Evonne last July she was going to elope with Miller Springstead, Evonne had said: "Oh my God! You're not serious? Are you, Lindsay?" Her small nose had wrinkled and her upper lip had drawn back unattractively. "I mean, God, Lindsay, if you have to run off with somebody, do it with Conrad Hilton...or Royal Bergeron or somebody..."

Lindsay had expected support: "E-*vonne*...you're such a...*snob*..."

"God, Lindsay, I've spent half my life figuring out how the hell I'm going to get out of this godawful backwater..."

"Well it's not like we're going to live in an old truck body in the junkyard, for God's sake—Miller's going to grad school at Iowa, which is a perfectly good school, it's in the Big Ten, for God's sake, and he's getting his PhD and I just really think you're being ..." Her lips had trembled: *Goddamn you, Evonne, we're friends...*

A nearly blinding flash from something in a fallow ditch to her right, the sun off a piece of chromed metal, perhaps, made her wince. She rummaged in the glove compartment and found a pair of her mother's sunglasses—Wyn owned many —and she put them on. They fit perfectly.

She slowed at that point on Highway 31, almost midpoint between the Noel home in Ermine Falls and the Shack on the lake, where the Springstead home and TURNER'S AUTO & TRUCK PARTS had been, and pulled off on the shoulder. She peered through the windshield, unable to bring herself to get out of the car. In any case, the Bide-A-Wee motel was now under construction, as the caterpillar and excavating going on behind the sign announcing the Bide-A-Wee's advent testified. There was nothing of Turner Springstead's home and business to be seen, save for a small apple orchard on a hill well up behind the current land work, which she had heard Miller refer to wistfully as the second most peaceful place he could think of. He wouldn't tell her the first—she thought it probably had something to do with making love. Almost squinting now, she could make out in the distance the trees in the orchard, the limbs twisted like misshapen arms—so it seemed to Lindsay as they came into focus—reaching after something successfully fleeing before them.

Behind the Bide-A-Wee's work-in-progress the nearest hills were lushly verdant and stacked in serpent coils of foliage, while in the more distant vista the air appeared faintly blue. God it was lovely, or it could be, this north country, if only you knew how to live in it or whatever.

Cedar Haven Road branched off 31 and followed the edge of Silverfish Lake, a long winding drive almost all downhill which went past the lake's more prominent summer homes, including the Noels'. And there it was, the first substantially modern cottage anyone'd built. She thought of herself and Miller, first shyly confessing their love after having known each other less than a week, how they'd made love the first time on the sleeping balcony, and herself, shameless, perhaps, for the first time in her life not (at least initially) resisting a boy's advances but joining him in the conspiracy to rend something her body wanted from the world. Her pulse quickened as she drove past; she almost wished she smoked, for it seemed the perfect moment for a cigarette.

*

J. Puckett it said on the mailbox. Evonne's house was tucked back behind a curtain of small supple birch like some drowsing animal known for natural camouflage. Hardly anybody in Michigan did their houses in cedar shakes and then let them weather naturally like so many of the houses in New England. The Puckett house seemed to rise from the ground on which it sat like a tree—beside it their "raised ranch" in Iowa seemed inhospitable as a concrete bunker. It was small but two stories, a summer cottage variation of a Cape Anne, with dormers like eyes peering from sharply angled slopes.

She got out. Steam rose in stringy webs from the hood of the Cutlass. She moved toward the screened porch. She could see a faintly swaying old-fashioned swing inside.

"Lindsay!" Evonne was at the door before she could knock, her hair in thick blonde braids, ruddier than she used to be, her belly swollen.

Evonne's warm fingers closed on her own and she was pulled into the screened porch, across it and into the house: "Come *in*, How are you, howhaveyou*been*?"

They sat on a sofa in the living room. The downstairs of the house was tri-chambered like a bird's heart into living room, dining room and kitchen. The walls were yellow and there was a sprightly systole-diastole cadence in the billowing out, then

145

lazy collapsing, of the living room curtains. The carpeting was mauve.

"Gee...I just love your house Evonne, the way it kind of *sprouts* here or something..."

"It does sit kind of low—there's no basement, you know."

"Really?" She couldn't recall having been in a house without a basement. Even the Shack had one.

"No—the place sits on thirteen concrete piers with metal posts set in them that're bolted to the frame, then the crawlspace's sealed up tight in the winter to protect the pipes under the floor..."

Lindsay started to cry and Evonne moved toward her, put her arms around her and comforted her.

"How long are you home for? Your mom said she didn't know..."

"I don't know."

"Oh...you know, I was just thinking the other day about how awful I was to you last summer, you know, when you first told me you were running away with Miller? Maybe I was just jealous. You were so cute and excited and when Miller came to get you in his jeans and sweater with his hair still wet and you both looked so happy and after you were gone I cried and cried and cried...just because..."

"Just because *why*?"

"Because there's nothing sad as the one who gets left behind, hell, I don't know, but it had something to do with the way Jerry and I got together. He's from Traverse, you know, he works for A & J Heating, and anyway he was at the Hills a little after you left working on the air conditioning...he asked me out, and somehow because I was so lonely 'cause you'd left, so instead of saying, Go peddle your papers, I said, Sure. And we went to the movies, then Jerry brought me out here, it was really just a summer cottage then and Jerry was working on it, winterizing it and he was going on about the heating and so forth. He'd brought a sixpack and some potato chips and we ate and drank and I felt this feeling creep over me like a blush, like something'd given way and I looked over at the windows there, I love tall windows, don't you, and I looked out at the lake, there were whitecaps and it looked cold as all get-out, and then in the top of my head I knew: this is what I want." She giggled and flopped against the sofa and massaged her child through her stomach. "However, I got a little more than I bargained for."

And so they talked: of the people from Ermine Falls they both knew, of Ermine Hills, the weather, how Evonne would finish college (with summer schools and extension courses), when the baby was due (mid-September), how Lindsay liked Iowa:

"...and the worst thing is not the heat but the humidity," she found herself saying.

"Lindsay...you haven't said much about Miller...is everything okay? You guys're basically okay, aren't you, it's just one of those things that come along from time to time, right? Tell me what's the matter, why don't you?"

"Sure, no, well, we're basically okay, it just gets tough sometimes, I—omigosh!"—she'd glanced at the clock on the mantel—"it's eleven-thirty already! I have to stop at the Shack on the way home, I absolutely *have* to be home for a lunch at one or Mom'll have kittens, I'm so sorry I have to leave now, Evonne..."

*

It was cool inside. The Shack had that alien odor of a house that hadn't been occupied for a while but which is cleaned periodically. She put on a Barracuta jacket she found draped across a chair and felt hungry. There was no food in the refrigerator but there was plenty of beer. She took a bottle of Lowenbrau to the sink where the foot-long bottle opener hung from its hook. Beyond the window the lake flashed in the sun like a pebbled mirror.

She wandered aimlessly back into the living room, sipping at the beer, pausing at the curving wrought-iron stairway that led to the sleeping balcony: and up there, with Miller M. Springstead, was where I discovered how much I really liked to fuck, and where I got almost instantly crazy for him. I think now because he had a kind of melancholy energy that I liked and I wanted to join him in whatever struggles were coming and God for all I know I finished the movement my hand had begun in the ninth grade toward that hideous Basil Purvis, but next to his strong body was where I wanted to be and then those short strong fingers clamped around my ankle...she felt tears in her eyes.

147

The she noticed the fireplace: a nice fire was laid in it. Why not? She could afford another half hour. She rolled a leather cushioned recliner chair of her father's before the fireplace, adjusted its back, stooped and lit the paper. She wrapped herself in an afghan, got on the chair, and waited for the snapping fire to really catch. Soon she could feel warmth, and it seemed to calm her and seep into her bones, soothing, narcotic.

*

On a night in Bay City long before she'd ever come to Ermine Falls, she was ten, twelve, something like that, she lay drowsing on a chaise longue on the patio, a soft summer evening shot with peepers and leg-fiddling nightbugs. From the house she could hear Bertha saying, "Uh-huh, uh-huh, uh-huh," into the telephone. From an upstairs window she heard her father's hi-fi playing one of his favorite Mills Brothers albums: *I love those dear hearts, and gentle people, who live and love in my home town...*

She nodded, drifted off, came back:

I feel so wel-come—each time that I return, That my happy heart keeps laughing like a clown...

Security covered her like some soft, fur-lined glove and she hugged her arms around herself, thinking, *Gee, I love us all...*

Then she was a junior at the U of M and still living with Aunt Roxy, though she could have stayed in a dorm, and she was still a virgin.

I was going to the Kappa house to return Cheryl Gumberg's zoology notes; it was lovely, drifting through the violet dusk, along the sidewalk past a row of fraternity houses...I came to one that was new and looked like a modernistic church, all brick and steel and lots of glass.

Standing there on the sidewalk in front of the house's lawn were a dozen sorority pledges, all about half-drunk and smoking cigarettes, giggling and poking each other. I was dressed like several of them in white Levis and Michigan sweatshirt, and I thought it'd be kind of funny to slip right in among them and see what was cooking. "*When?*" someone whispered.

"Pretty soon now, I just hope...I can't *stand* waiting—Marjorie, give me a Salem?"

148

I pressed my books against my chest and there we all stood, rubbernecking at the house like anxious geese. The darkened house was lit only by some amber glow within, but then at last the top lit up like a pinball machine, there were winking Christmas lights all around the biggest gable on the third floor where I guess the dorm part was...and there, beautifully framed in the huge triangular window, were the naked behinds of ten men, four on the bottom rank, three on top of them, then two, then one last one crouched shakily athwart the pyramid formed by the others, his rear pointed toward us like some perky white flower, his parts reduced by distance and lighting to something like a shapeless tail.

"Oh wow, a pyramid moon," a gigantic-breasted brunette breathed, "isn't that fan*tas*tic, oh, wow..."

Two behind me broke into hysterical laughter.

"Oh, *no*," someone corrected Big Tits and I turned to see another girl in sweatshirt and jeans, a little dark-haired girl with eyes round and large as golfballs behind glasses with magnifying lenses. "That isn't it at *all*," she said scornfully, "what you're looking at is *much* more elaborate, that's not just another pyramid moon—*look*, look what they're doing—" And sure enough the whole triangle of nude limbs in the distance was moving, quivering, and with incredible control the whole entity of asses moved until at last the buttocks of each man were pressed flush against the windows. "You see," said the small girl triumphantly, "that's a pyramid *pressed-ham!*"

Then they all moved down the street leaving me there.

"Hi, you're Lindsay, aren't you? Remember me?"

"Oh. Hi. You're...Royal, right?"

Before she faced him fully, she noted that the pressed-ham that had been so impressive had crumpled to nothingness.

Where'd she met Royal Bergeron? Oh, yeah: about two weeks ago at the Union at the table with Cheryl. He was a Deke and they were notorious as cocksmen and boozers, though not in a muscular, jock-house kind of way like the SAEs and ATOs; they were what you'd call "remission men at this end of the century," a helpful Sigma Chi she'd once dated had told her. She could tell he'd liked her looks and he'd said he'd call her up—but he hadn't, which was just as well, as she'd all the dates just now her studying could afford.

They fell in step, walking in the general direction of the Union. Royal was a bit plump but he had a face that was clean and fresh as a Red Delicious cut in half, though his dominant expression seemed one of supercilious arrogance. He had short dark hair and a wonderfully clear complexion with long lashes. He played volleyball a lot and was from Grosse Pointe which meant, Lindsay supposed, that he was probably rich. Certainly he had that indolent look about him that all the rich kids she'd known had seemed to have.

"That was some spectacle," he said. "I didn't know you were pledging. What's the story behind that display?"

"I'm not pledging, I was just standing there for the fun of it. Wasn't that something?" She mimicked the goggle-eyed girl: "Oh, wow, a pressed ham, isn't that just too, too much!"

Royal laughed appreciatively. "Yeah, sophomoric indeed, in deed as well as reality...how about a beer?"

"Gee, thanks...but I should get home, I have to study..."

"A townie, eh? Remember, study is the curse of the drinking class."

"Oh, I suppose I could...but my aunt'd probably get steamed up..."

"Your aunt?" He said "ahnt" like a New Englander. She remembered Cheryl'd said he'd gone to prep school at St. George's in Rhode Island, so maybe that explained it.

"Uh-huh. I come from the northern part of the state—at least now I do, I'm originally from Bay City—up around Traverse City, but I went to high school here—University High."

"Must be sort of a drag to have to live with your aunt."

"Oh...not really. She's real nice. She's a widow and almost sixty, but she's really funny and enthusiastic...she substitutes for housemothers at the sorority houses sometimes..."

"But still kind of dull, huh?"

"Why do you say that?" Because indeed Roxanne Noel Braintree, young for her age, quick-witted, liberal, a fund of information whether you wanted it or not, was kind of dull, and she made Lindsay antsy because she was always slipping noiselessly around in her Norwegian slipper socks to see if she could help Lindsay in some way.

"Oh, something in your look, I guess. Look, come on, let's hop in my hearse, it's close by, we'll nip down to the P-Bell for a beer

150

and conversation, don't worry if you're not quite twenty-one, I know the people there."

"Do you really have a hearse?"

"Sure. It's parked over behind the Union: a forty-eight Caddy completely restored, complements of my old man, he works for GM—who doesn't in Michigan—and he gave it to me in anticipation of the graduation I was supposed to be in last year but didn't quite make due to this little matter of flunking bio the for the second time. Made it the third time this year, though, so looks like I'll be free...free to go to work or whatever the hell people do when they get out. But first, of course, I'm going to take what they used to call the Grand Tour of Europe..."

"A hearse?"

"Yup."

"Neat."

*

In two weeks I took Royal home to Ermine Falls for a long weekend just before graduation. He loved it. And Mom loved him because he was so courtly and well-mannered and well-dressed and oozed a kind of attractive carelessness, yet always was entirely attentive whenever he was talking to Mom or Daddy. Who also liked him, though he was a little more cautious because he noticed Royal was never entirely sober the whole while...though of course he was never really drunk either.

On the way back to Ann Arbor he asked me to wear his fraternity pin: "I mean, I don't want to push you into anything, so forget the engaged-to-be-engaged implication and just consider it a token of my affection, or even just as a pretty ornament for your pretty chest and because I guess I love you." This last he said almost sorrowfully and his eyes were lovely and dark and who could resist that?

Aunt Roxy thought I was coming back the next day, so it turned out that that night I lay on Royal's bed in his apartment on the corner of Hill and Packard, wearing one of his oxford cloth shirts and nothing else, and I thought back to how I'd come to Ann Arbor and Aunt Roxy in the first place, and for a moment I almost hated Daddy for letting me come.

I looked over at Royal. He was naked, on his back, and his

151

mouth was open and his arms and legs thrown wide. His body hair shaded him like chiaroscuro in a drawing. It was hot and muggy and in the light from a street light his mouth was a black hole. Suddenly he seemed alien, as if it had been a stranger who'd put a spell on me and brought me here and undressed me and made his gentle and anticlimactic entrance into me and now I didn't know whether to feel happy or sad that it was over at last.

As I lay there in the semi-dark, I felt a grin twist my lips and knew I had that look that Mom hated and always made her say that thing about swallowing the canary; it tugged at the corners of my mouth and I thought, Well, Kiddo, losing your virginity was not such a big deal, was it? Thanks, Royal, I guess this is what friends are for, huh?

Once in spring of my senior year Royal and I were both a little drunk, parked out by the Arb, I could feel the greenness even in the dark, it was raining, we were making out on the mattress in the back of the hearse, How queer, I thought, to be thus engaged where maybe hundreds of corpses had lain before us over the years...

Royal was warm against me, the windows were cracked a bit but still misted from our exertions. "Oh God, I love you, sweets," Royal muttered. The radio was playing a Ray Coniff version of "Blue Velvet"...

But then I wasn't in the hearse, I was lying nude and on display on something like wet velvet and somehow I was in the back of Daddy's huge black Olds and when the driver turned it wasn't Royal or Daddy but Miller, looking back at me with that horrid wolfish grin he gets sometimes, he grinned wider and wider as the mouth of a big black-ribbed tunnel I could see through the windshield we were driving into got closer and closer, arching above us—

—Something nudged her in a pleasant direction, away from the terrifying tunnel: it was another time at night, she and Miller were outside the Shack on the sandy beach in their bare feet and the little waves coming in made gulping sounds.

We stood looking up into the huge inverted bowl of night brimming with stars, I thought of all the years it took the light to get here to strike our retinas and I brought the cold tart umpteenth can of beer to my lips, clicking my teeth against the edge. Miller wore a sweater and chinos and looked as collegiate as could be and he held me tight against him and I thought about what a good afternoon we'd had: Paul Dugald, whom I'd once gone out with and who was at Harvard, had taken us out in the Dugald Chris-Craft with a tub of iced beer and we kept making stupid jokes when one of us'd have to jump overboard to whiz and then we came back to shore bumping over the pebbly waves in the fat inboard and my skin got goosebumps: We were going to Iowa City in three days, yippee!

She awoke on the chaise before the fireplace in the Shack. It was 1:30 the clock on the mantel said. "God-damnit." She felt awful, groggy, cranky as she used to as a kid when roused from her nap. Wyn would not be happy—Wyn would have kittens.

The fire which had started so promisingly and had lulled her to sleep had not, she noticed, really burned very well after all: the charred logs, still almost whole, were smoldering, and hissed as worms of red corruscated on their surfaces, darted here and there like frantic waterbugs, flared, and winked out.

TWELVE

In February of my senior year at Central State I drove my VW to Ann Arbor one evening to go hear an *Esquire*-sponsored literary symposium where Nelson Algren and William Styron and some others I'd been reading were going to be holding forth...but as with various other of my enterprises, something thwarted me: on some obscure urge, I took along two pint bottles of Jim Beam and had completely swilled one by the time I pulled up behind the U of M Union.

After a few nips out of the second pint, I figured it was time to ask somebody where Angell Hall was, but somehow I fell in with a group of roisterers going to a fraternity party and somehow I followed them right into the house. It was one of those big mothers, not far from the union, that was all sunken floors and deep carpet and dorms upstairs where all the frat rats would be pronging their dates later on, I presumed...live rock music, thick purple velvet curtains over monstrous windows, people, sweaty, drunk, milling around, all this going on at the same time like some freaky vision out of Hieronymous Bosch, and here I was, by the dance floor, standing there like the veriest of swamp rats in my heavy parka and my pacs, weaving around, not bothering to find the source of drinks in the place but every now and then taking out my pint and having a nip. As the rock music blared on, couples around me jerked and twitched like they were being juiced with electricity, making me think of how a guinea hen'd be with a weasel after it.

I came, finally, to focus on this big tall guy, probably a basketball player from the look of assurance his face wore and his body projected, dancing up a storm with a cute little blond girl a little over five feet tall, just about my size, the top of her head'd just come to my chin, and God how I drunkenly yearned for her with her compact body and perky tits under a powder blue sweater and golden lovely hair cut short in a page-boy bob so it bounced and fell over her china-blue eyes. She glanced at me from time to time with what I took for interest and I looked back with no doubt naked yearning. And the guy seemed to have remarked me too, the way two potential antagonists spot each other in a gin mill: for every time they danced near me, the guy would maneuver himself close so he could bump into me as I stood there swaying, and I'd mutter "Sorry," and he'd look down and scowl as if to say, Get the fuck out of here, peasant...

A slow dance began to "Blue Moon" with revolving colors on the overhead spotlight painting the couples with red, then green, then gold, and the lights made the guy's tiny fraternity pin twinkle. He wore a soft gray cashmere sweater and checkered pants and calfskin boots, and I guess I just stood there open-mouthed, gawking in country-boy wonderment: for this was the archetype, the guy out of he ads, the one leaning on his MG, his London Fog tossed casually over an arm as he waits for the Sweetheart of Sigma Chi to come floating down the steps of the Kappa Kappa Gamma house trailing such clouds of femininity that even the chops of a confirmed misogynist would involuntarily slaver.

I seemed unable to pull my gaze from them, could only gawk like the yokel I was. They drifted toward me again—*Without a dream in my heart, without a love of my ownnnn*—and this time the guy was carrying a half-full pitcher of beer, which he held behind the blond's back...they got closer until the guy towered over me and I looked up: he must have been at least six-five, with delicate arrogant features and a great mop of curly copper-gold hair. "You zany little poop," he said. "You pestiferous knave, you oddity, you buffoon, you party-crashing churl."

He brought the hand with the beer mug in it around from behind the girl's back, raised it high, and poured it down into my upturned face. "Knave, varlet, bumpkin, lout..." he intoned boredly

The beer slopped over my face and ran down the front of the parka Turner'd got me for Christmas five years earlier and over my pacs and I stood stock-still except for a little weaving...and then began to lower down into a kind of crouch to get away from the stream of beer.

I happened to glance into the face of the little blond: and saw this faint, bewildered semi-smile of horror on her sweet lips, as if she'd been stunned by seeing an animal killed in traffic.

It must have taken a couple of seconds for rage to shake

hands with the alcohol in my system. And then I drove up out of my crouch on legs that I'd been keeping in shape by doing one-leg squats while holding a fifty-pound dumbell, both my arms extending upward and my hands opening to rend, tear, break—

We crashed to the floor with my hands around his neck, squeezing, I thought I felt something give in his throat—

—Then the hands, from all over, were pulling, trying to peel me off this gorgeous tall bastard who'd toppled like a crumbling steeple when my hands'd closed around his neck, and when I realized I couldn't hang on any longer and had anyway choked him half to death, I quick let go and had just enough time to fetch him a solid right dead center in the mouth that his dentist's still probably repairing, then went flying back into the whole pack of them, hitting, kicking, kneeing, butting, even biting someone on the hand once, finally getting myself clear and hot-footing it out the main door and into the night—

*

I awaken around six, flat on my back in my underwear, on the study Hideabed. Hangover is skulking around the fringes of my consciousness like some shit-eating dog, so I take a can of Budweiser into the shower with me and let the hot water beat down. The Ann Arbor incident I think may have been on my mind when I came back to Ermine Falls from Mount Haven in June to sign the various papers at the closing for the house and land and all the cars and trucks and whatnot— twelve grand for the whole kit and kaboodle, just a few grand more than what Turner paid for it when he came back from the war, but I was hardly in a mood for bargaining.

Later I went to the Hills and took a room and said I'd be there for three days, though that stretched into a week once I'd met auburn-haired long-legged high-titted Lindsay Noel and found she could actually reciprocate what I tried to keep from being obvious: my almost instant adoration. So like the nameless college girl at the frat party, or a girl named Sandy Dehner I met at Les Champs du Roi back when I was 18, I was pulled by attraction like iron filings to a magnet; I knew I should have flown but was helpless.

But anyhow, there I was at the Hills, with several hundred

156

dollars in cash and a check for twelve grand. And naturally to celebrate I'd bought a bottle of good sauce, Old Grandad, and soon I was sprawled on the flawlessly made bed of room 202 at Ermine Falls without a stitch on, playing with the money, which was spread out on the bed in front of me. And lying off to the side was Turner's old Steyr pistol which I'd taken to carrying in the VW.

I was poking the money around, as much cash as I'd ever seen in one place, forming patterns with it. I wasn't fondling the crap, just looking at it in wonderment: there it was, these little scraps of paper negotiable in practically any corner of the world, the wherewithal that puts others over or under you, and the simple fear of not having which could reach into you and clutch you like a hand precariously holding and kneading your heart, lights and balls.

I touched the pistol; I hadn't brought it for protection but to help me decide: should I use it to kill Bernard Dunstable, he who killed my brother—and by extension, my father?

This was how I'd finally figured to do it. I'd drive out to Dunstable's house trailer where he lived alone and a little before he got back after his night shift—it'd be around five in the morning—and pull around where I couldn't be seen from the road. He'd drive around to his back door and see the VW, where I'd be slumped over the wheel. He'd come over for a look and seeing me there as though passed out, he'd pull open my door— and I would put the barrel of the Steyr about a foot from his face and touch it off. It'd be a snap to slam one round dead center in his face, step out, administer a quick coup de grace, recover my two shells, pull forward, obscure my car tracks, then light out, chucking the pistol and my cotton gloves (to foil a paraffin test: I hadn't read a million Perry Masons for nothing), and haul ass back to Iowa never to return.

The trouble was not to do with my fear of getting caught or with uncertainty about whether or not my sinew would stand me in good stead when the moment of truth arrived; it had to do with Burner's face: it was mean, stupid, loathsome, vile...but was it evil? Was that head foreman to a crew of limbs devoted to hurting and maiming just for the joy of being malignant, or was Bernard Dunstable really, as Turner had suggested, no worse than a weasel in a henhouse?

157

So there I was, sprawled out bare ass getting potted and pondering these weighty matters and I thought, well, let's go downstairs and get some chow, no point in plotting murder most foul on an empty stomach. And I showered and dressed and went to the dining room and was waited on by Lindsay Noel, who'd known Rex briefly, so she said, and who agreed to ride over to Traverse City with me and go to the little summer playhouse. So that was what I'd done instead of murdering Burner Dunstable—and that was our beginning and, as well, all she wrote for my mad scheme of revenge, which went a-glimmering that very night—no doubt just as well, no matter how you cut it.

*

I throw on the blue terrycloth robe Lindsay gave me for Christmas, turn on the TV with the volume off, loll back on the Hideabed; the beer isn't keeping Mister Hangover far enough away from me; I pour a couple ounces of Beam in a water glass and quaff it, then chase it. That's a little better.

*

Lindsay and I became inseparable and after three days we made love. I remember that day coming down to have lunch by the pool. She was off duty so she came up with her suit on and suggested we have lunch at the Noel "shack" on Silverfish Lake.

Sure. But before I went up to my room to put on some jeans and a shirt, we went hand in hand, skipping almost, to the pool, and we rose into the air together out over the cool water. I could have lived in that moment of glorious suspension for the rest of my life.

Some "shack": a spacious A-frame cottage with four bed-rooms and a huge sun deck from which you could step onto the dock and in about five running steps dive into the lake. The place was all rough-hewn overhead beams and knotty pine and car-peting and acres of windows and sliding glass doors.

We sat at the kitchen table and you served us up some cold chicken and potato salad and Lowenbrau as you chattered on about the guy named Royal you'd broken up with and his pal Randy who was trying to be a poet who'd got the hots for you after Royal and I smiled my best smile and tried to keep up my projection of myself as yours truly, the doctoral candidate, the up-by-his-bootstraps boy who in spite of grief over the recent deaths of brother and father was determined to bravely do well in the nasty old world.

Her voice: calm but ready to get excited, throaty with a sort of shy tentativeness, not quite diffidence, like it really wanted to say (but of course wouldn't): You were right, Miller, there *is* something going on with us, isn't there? In short, I found it just plain thrilling: "What I mean is, Miller, you shouldn't stay *here* much longer and squander your money, I mean how can you like this here with all these kind of spoiled and, oh, pretentious *jerks*, or at least the way most of them are?..."

"Oh, I know, I know. But I've just always had this kind of itch to come here and when the opportunity to scratch came along I thought, what the hell, I don't know much, but seems to me I've seen the folly of *deferring* things...anyhow, couple of days I'll be off for Iowa and maybe close the deal on the little two-bedroom house I was telling you about. I want to get the money I do have into something where it'll be safe and doing something for me...and when that deal's concluded maybe instead of staying there and reading I'll come back to Michigan one last time: to see you...if you'd like me to, that is...to see if I can resist tucking you under my arm and taking you off to the land of hogs and cornfields with me..." I couldn't tell if I maintained the right degree of lightness in my voice or not; I think it shook just a bit in its effort to be casual.

After we'd swum in the lake, Lindsay lit a fire in the living room fireplace. It was getting toward evening and there was just enough of a nip in the air to make it worthwhile; soon the rich smell of smoke from seasoned applewood was around us and we were flopped before the flames side by side. We both took off the U of M sweatshirts she'd got us after the swim and rolled them up for pillows and lay there, belly-down and side by side like drowsing dogs, our chins on our forearms, she in her bikini, I in my trunks, staring into the fire. "Speaking of pretension"—I felt close enough to her to speak like this—"calling this place the 'shack' is a technique I find interesting..."

159

"Yeah. Sometimes it seems unreal to me, and transitory, like it's waiting for a strong wind to come along and carry it off...Miller?"

"Hmmmm?"

"Tell me about the PhD—why you want it. Do you really feel like you have, oh, a *call* or something to be a teacher...or do critical work or something? What do you *want*, I mean *ultimately*? Is it the challenge that's making you go for it?"

I edged closer to her in spite of the heat of the fire. And like a fool, maybe, instead of saying, I want to contribute to the world, or quoting something like, A Teacher Affects Eternity, or some such crap, I tried the truth out on her: "For its own sake. I guess deep down I want the PhD so I can have one thing of value that nobody can take away from me, and once got, I could commit a pair of grisly axe murders like old Raskolnikov or, hell, any of a practically infinite number of outrages, but even if pitched into the abyss, I'd still be Miller Springstead, PhD...I could have it writ on my tombstone. Challenge, hell. What I reckon I really want, *ultimately* as you put it, is a little peace, serenity, call it what you will: to have each day be neither horrid nor wonderful but just like the days before and the days to come...*challenge* is just another word for contention, far's I'm concerned, and I've already had all of that I want..."

Perplexed, Lindsay tossed her hair, still damp, to spread it forward like some dark red exotic fan for the fire to dry; what I could see of her face was dark orange in the light from the shifting flames and I almost blurted out, *I love you, could you ever consider marrying me?*

While your face was still cloudy from thinking over what I'd said, I twisted around and took your foot in my hand. I bent your knee and brought your foot, then, close to my face like it was a bowl brimming with roses, I cupped your heel and pressed my lips against the side of your foot; it was tanned over the instep and almost microscopic red-blonde hairs flowered on each toe and I thought I could feel your flesh throb against my lips as I tasted your salt on my tongue. We both sat up, then, and you came easily into my embrace, your mouth half-parted, your tongue and lips like firm and slightly underripe fruit and as the moments slipped on you became rosy with desire.

As we climbed the winding wrought-iron staircase up to the

160

sleeping balcony, I was shivering and atingle and forced myself to keep my eyes off the movement of your bikini-clad hips.

We lay on the carpeted floor, not bothering with making it to a bed.

Inside her I couldn't have lasted for more than half a minute and as I nearly fainted she clutched me tighter and groaned in something between fear and elation and something else.

We lay joined and quiescent for some long slack lovely moments, and then I could feel the engines of sex rekindling within us, your slick silky-ribbed muscles tightening spasmodically around me every time I swelled another millimetre. You whispered in about the smallest voice I'd ever heard, "Did you mean that about carrying me off to Iowa?"

"Yes. I do believe I love you," I whispered. God! Did I really say that? I pressed my lips against your dampish hair, used my nose to burrow through it and find your ear with its cool rim, then kissed your feverish face and helplessly murmured again, "I love you," and you didn't say anything and I swelled some more inside you and your breathing quickened and I held you ever more tightly, stiffening to my fullest distension, feeling impossibly virile and large inside you. "Me too," you whispered back.

THIRTEEN

Miller and I drove back to Ermine Falls the day after we'd driven to Petoskey and been married by a funny little JP—I'd always like Petoskey, especially for the clothes sales near the end of the summer season, and just after we were married, before we went and found a motel, we walked for a little while, hand-in-hand, hardly speaking, along the shore of Little Traverse Bay. Miller found several Petoskey stones and gave me a wonderfully-patterned oval one to keep as a lucky piece. He'd carried one in his pocket himself since he was seventeen.

I'd called Daddy from the Hills before we left; Mom'd insisted on a small church wedding of some kind, and wouldn't let us have a wedding at the Shack (if we could have gotten rid of the guests afterward, we could have continued right into our little honeymoon up on the sleeping loft), damn her anyway. So we did it our way. Actually Miller, with his eyes already on the more distant vistas of the coming year in Iowa, was more or less indifferent to *how* we did it at all—for him it was like signing a contract, probably from coming from a womanless home, I surmised. However, I didn't care either: however we did it as long as we did it and did it quick was fine with me too.

And so yesterday in the bar at the Hills I had another Bloody Mary with Miller. Then we went to his room and made love. Then I called Daddy and said, "Daddy, Miller and I are eloping." And why shouldn't we do what we'd talked about: we had our license, our blood tests to prove we weren't syphlitic, we were both, as Daddy liked to say, lecturing me about my various responsibilities, free, white and over twenty-one.

There was a silence, then he said: "Oh, Christ."

"Yes. Well."

"Listen, honey, your mother'll be fit to be...she'll be absolutely livid..."

I stuck my bare foot on Miller's, twisted it, wormed my toes between his, cheered beyond measure that Daddy hadn't started off by telling me just how impossible it was for me to do what I was telling him I was going to do. It was hard to sit still there with the phone clamped to my ear. I felt antsy, I wanted to leave now for my new world, up to now everything'd been a preparation for life: now I was ready to get on with living. So I said: "Well, I'm sorry, but I can't help it about Mom, we'll just never see eye-to-eye on anything no matter what, and I—we, Miller and me, we just can't *take* a church wedding and hurry-up invitations and all the rest, and besides Miller doesn't really have any family any more and we'd just as soon do it the way we're going to do it..."

"Your mother'll say, Well, that just proves she was pregnant all the time," Daddy said uneasily.

"Well, I'm not, so what do I care," I said haughtily, "let her think what she wants."

"Honey, I'm very full of doubts myself..."

"Why?"

"Well...maybe uneasy is the better word. I guess all whirlwind courtships, so to speak, trouble me. Christ, look at the mistakes people make even after they have a mutual history to give them some indication they're compatible. I wonder if you have any idea what's in...oh, hell, well, I suppose I'm just a naysaying old fart who hates to lose his only child even when I suppose it's a reasonable time for her to leave the nest. And naturally I'd distrust any guy who was taking her from me. But what the hell, you're free, white and over twenty-one, as the fellow says, you've got a college education. I gather Miller's had some pretty miserable times, poor kid, I know how tough the father-brother thing'd be on anybody. But oftentimes those are the people who go on to lead exemplary lives and give their own kids what they missed, you see...I'm rambling, aren't I? Well, hell, you two kids *should* have all you need to make a go of it...and if you don't it'll turn out to be the fault of your own shortsightedness...you know what I mean?"

My concentration was pretty weak, and I didn't really have the faintest idea, but I said, "Yes." Now Miller was behind me, gently massaging my naked back, kissing the spot between my shoulderblades.

"I have to go, Daddy."

There was another long silence, then Daddy said in a choked voice, "God, I wish you the best of everything."

163

"Thanks."

"One other thing, honey?"

"Uh-huh, sure..."

"I've never felt more alone in my life, but I don't think I'm exactly sad, either. Tell Miller congratulations, he's the luckiest man alive."

His love and sudden loneliness seemed to flow along the wires and into me like painless needles and I thought, Oh Daddy, don't feel bad.

All I could say was, "Thanks and I love you and Mom too and I'll see you both sometime tomorrow, probably later in the day, and tell Uncle Milton I'm sorry because I know he was looking forward to a real wedding..." I hung up quickly and turned and pressed myself gratefully against Miller and my tears leaked onto his strong shoulders and he comforted me gently, kissing the skin where it was wet, saying "There, there, it'll all turn out okay, Lindsay, you'll see, it's us against the world and we'll do okay, you'll see..."

*

And the next afternoon when Mr. and Mrs. Miller Springstead pulled up in the drive in Miller's VW, Daddy was out the front door, waving awkwardly, beaming, coming up to us with almost unintelligible cries of affection and greeting, kissing me, hugging me, squeezing Miller's hand as he got out of the car, once even pounding him on the back. Miller looked a little sheepish and I knew he was grateful for this garrulity. He looked as though he were about to apologize, so I tried to ease things along by hooking my arms through both theirs and prattling on: "Oh Daddy, you should have seen the neat little JP who married us in Petoskey, he looked like an elf and he had a nose like a potato, and while we went through the ceremony there was this big picture window behind him and we could look out and see Little Traverse Bay all frothy with whitecaps while we took our vows..."

Daddy took my cue and began to get a little caught up in the spirit of the thing; I think we were both trying to keep Mom's absence from being oppressive. Then Daddy was inviting us in—how absurd it sounded to be invited into your own house—telling us he'd chilled some champagne, that he was sorry as hell Wyn

164

couldn't come down right now, she had one of those splitting migraines she got and she'd taken some Cafergot and that'd made her woozy and she was, as Daddy said, "out like a light."

As we walked up the front walk, Daddy began to talk animatedly to Miller about the Volvo station wagon sitting in the drive, though he'd not yet told us it was our wedding gift.

I loosened the grip I had on both my men and walked a little behind as Daddy continued to sell Miller the Volvo he was going to give us.

Later, after we'd drunk some champagne, Daddy thought about chucking the glasses into the fireplace, but we didn't because neither of us could tell whether or not they were Mom's good ones that she'd gotten as a wedding gift twenty-five years earlier or if they were just, as Daddy said, "for utility's sake."

*

A little later on Miller set about selling his VW and getting the U-Haul truck arranged and I tagged along with him.

The next morning, after I'd packed my clothes and stereo and records and things into big cardboard boxes that Miller'd carry down to the truck, I heard a noise and opened the door of my room a crack and looked out into the hallway. Mom came out of her room walking very carefully in her blue robe; she looked either drunk or drugged or both. I saw her step over to the window and look down upon the drive where the orange and white U Haul truck would have been. Then she did the strangest thing: she cleared her throat with a harsh, masculine sound, and spat on the carpeted floor of the hall. Then she turned and stepped back into her room. After the door shut I heard the lock click. In case I decided to force my way in and say good-bye? I laughed low in my throat and almost spat on the floor myself.

Then I ran downstairs to tell Daddy goodbye and to drive off in our new Volvo wagon with Miller; we had a rendez-vous at a garage Miller knew to get a tow bar so we could pull the Volvo behind the truck all the way to Iowa. "That way we won't start out separated," Miller explained.

The last thing Daddy called out before we headed out for Iowa around noontime was, *"Remember, we'll see you Christmas if not before—come Thanksgiving if you can!"*

*

Christmas! After a week of arguing and fighting, it came to a head two days before I wanted us to leave Iowa and go home for Christmas: "Miller, *please!*" Even I didn't like the whiny quality that had come into my voice.

"Goddamnit, I am *not* going to fucking Ermine Falls for Christmas, I can't, for the reasons I keep repeating to you..."

"Selfish! Hateful! You just don't give a damn about anything but me-me-me, do you? And I don't care about your damn *comps*—God, I hate that word—and you and your damned papers. You *knew* from the very day we got married I was counting on going home, that my folks wanted us both to come home for Christmas. I'd think you'd be grateful to have a family to have Christmas with. Those cheery little notes and things Mom's been sending are a good sign, she wants to patch things up. I promised Daddy!"

"Well, you may have, palzie-walzie, but I didn't and I am *not* gonna go off and leave this house empty to where I feel like I escaped from anyhow. This house is all we really own, lock, stock and barrel, it's our investment and capital all in one, it's got to be decently cared for so we can sell it for a decent price when we make the next step of our journey—I trust you don't want to hang around here and be a hopped-up pizza waitress for the rest of your life. And I have *got* to do those papers and keep up my reading, I still have to take finals after vacation, for Christ's sake—"

"That again! And again and again! So it'll be just like Thanksgiving when I drove home all alone and you stayed here and probably you were drunk all the time—"

"—Listen, your damn folks just want me there 'cause they'll think it's unseemly if I don't show up—there's sure as hell nothing in *my* character that makes 'em yearn for my presence. Don't worry so much, you'll all do just fine if I ain't there to nod and bow and scrape and ooh and ahh over sweaters and slippers and shaving lotion and crap like that. To hell with it, I know what a *real* Christmas is all about..."

"Hateful." And I threw my half cup of tepid tea in his face.

He jumped up from the sofa, tea dripping from his face and running down his sweatshirt front, cursing: "Goddamn fucking

166

nouveau-riche mountebanks with your goddamn bullshit pretentiousness...you're nothing but a bunch of phillistines, a bunch of asshole snotty vulgarians—"

"Vulgarians!" I crowed. "You should talk, you clodhopper with the vile filthy mouth!"

He drew back his hand, the fingers and palm stiffening into something like a paddle.

"Swamp-rat!" I hissed at him, shrinking nonetheless from the raised hand even as I baited him. "Unspeakable lout! Hillbilly! Farmer! Prick! Jerk!"

His hand lowered and he began to laugh, but it was only to himself and I felt more alone than ever.

*

Eight days later I drove up and parked in front of our house on Center Avenue and wondered what I would find. Maybe he'd be gone. Or dead drunk. Or something worse, whatever that might be. I'd come back laden with all kinds of gifts for Miller from my parents, and probably even he couldn't have foretold the number of sweaters—ten.

I opened the door. The house was more immaculate than I could ever had made it, Miller was bright and shining, his hair still damp from the shower. He was clear-eyed and crackling with energy as he pulled me joyously into his embrace, whirling me off my feet, dizzyingly around and around until we collapsed on the sofa, giggling. A cheerful fire was burning sturdily and on the mantel in a child's plastic sand bucket filled with ice a bottle of Taylor Brothers champagne was chilling.

There was one tricky part: as Miller carried me to the bedroom, I told him we couldn't, it was the wrong time. Then I said we shouldn't because it would get messy.

"I love anything that's you," he said into my hair. And so we plucked each other's clothes away and hurled them at the walls as if they were champagne glasses.

167

FOURTEEN

"Mom'll have kittens," Lindsay'd told Evonne when she'd stressed how important it was for her to be prompt: but when she first saw her mother's face on her return from the Shack, the figure of speech didn't seem so fancifully absurd. For some reason, Wyn's face made Lindsay think of how a hot biscuit looked just after it was broken open.

"Lindsay." Flat, declaritive, Wyn's voice also housed a quiver from the strain her poise was costing her.

"Hi, Mom, gee, I'm really—*rilly*—sorry I'm late, Mom, the thing is, I was over at Evonne's and we talked on and on about this and that for a long time, then I stopped off at the Shack to look for my old canvas MSU beer jacket that Larry Pringle gave me years ago, I *did* find it, thank goodness, though I forgot to bring it...but I guess I just lost all track of time...I hope that minister guy wasn't too disappointed, but I really don't need any advice any more, Daddy gave me a good talking-to last night...anyhow, I know Hilary makes such good lunches that'll have been its own reward...like virtue's s'posed to be, huh?..."

"Lindsay..."

"Oh, listen, let's talk about it in a minute, huh, I just really have to go to the bathroom, but really..." She did an urgent though specious little dance of impatience around her mother, forcing Wyn to turn awkwardly; and she slipped past her mother, moving quickly, and gained the stairs; her hand was on the bannister and her foot rising for the next step when her mother's voice halted her: *"Lindsay!"*

Lindsay turned, one foot still poised over a step: "Mom..."

"My dear, I am trying to remain as calm as possible but"— as if in response to to some unseen prompter's cue, one coiling tendril of beautiful silver hair unwound itself from her mother's coif and slid over her forehead—*"how could you do this to me?"*

"Well, my goodness, Mom, it's not the end of the *world*

or anything, I mean I'm sorry, I'm sorry I wasn't here to talk to this character, I just lost track of time like I said, but it wasn't necessary anyhow, I think I've figured out how things are and what to do on my own...Daddy helped me clarify things too, of course..."

"Lost track of time," Wyn snorted. "Lost track, my eye. You *distinctly* knew Reverend Dalyrimple would be here and his counseling might just have done you some small good, but you just couldn't *stand* the thought of that, could you, my dear. And after all the work poor Hilary went through to make things a success, *my dear...*"

"Where's Daddy, is he home yet?"

"Don't you try to distract me, my dear. And Hilary'd made this perfectly exquisite Beef Wellington and it wasn't very good after we'd waited forty-five minutes for her highness to arrive and the crust got all icky from meat juice..." Smirnoff's, her mother's favorite, might be "breathless" as the ads said, but Lindsay'd been around enough to tell when Wyn'd had a few.

"Lindsay, I demand a real apology, 'cause I've just had it up to here"—Wyn jerked a finger across her throat—"with your only child antics. At your age! Married! You've just always thought you were lucky as an elf, haven't you? How *dare* you, you and your icky junkman's son! The idea!"

Hilary had come in alarm from the kitchen and was approaching Wyn cautiously from the rear, as though to catch her should she topple backwards.

"Well?"

"Well, Mother, look: I didn't *ask* you to bring that counselor jerk or whoever here to meddle with me." She wanted desperately to get to her room and shut the door.

"Why...why, you just listen to me, you...you *snip*, you only child—"

"And I don't, I distinctly don't, Mother, want that wishy-washy Norman Vincent Peale stuff shoved down my throat either, I mean I know you have my best interests at heart and all that, and thanks for leaving that book in my room but I—"

"—How *dare* you?" Wyn moved closer, breathy, pungent. "How dare you, Little Miss Only Child, yes, I left that book for you, just maybe if there were more Reverend Dalyrimples and Norman Vincent Peales and Earl Nightingales around to ac-

169

centuate the positive maybe we wouldn't have such things as Little Miss Brat having to high-tail it home to her father at the first sign of trouble...and who might I ask is this Randy person? Is he that one that came up and stayed at the Shack that time with Royal Bergeron? Anyway, this Randy person called earlier and was talking all this rot about how he just *had* to see you, he said, and I *quote*, 'Tell her everything's okay and I care a lot for her and I have some good news for her.' So is this what you've become, some kind of *tramp*? Is *that* what this is really all about? Well: I'm waiting for an answer, Only Child."

Hilary caught a glimpse of Lindsay's crimson face and apparently finding the fare too rich began edging back away from the stair.

Lindsay's next words came easily to her lips, as if she'd been reserving them for the right occasion, and her voice was icy and contemptuous: "Stick it, Mother, just shove it." She wished Miller were here to hear her.

Wyn's slap came with surprising speed and force: she struck Lindsay high on the cheek, knocking her head to one side with a smack like a butcher's palm on a slab of meat.

Lindsay was too stunned to move, except to raise a wondering hand slowly to her warming cheek; Wyn jerked back with a little faltering step as though she'd been struck a blow, raising both arms protectively over her chest.

Lindsay suppressed an urge to shriek, *You dirty old bitch, I hate you!* and instead took a few seconds to compose herself. Then in her most freezing, condescending voice, she spoke to her mother, tilting her chin arrogantly out: "I really don't think this is a very *mature* reponse, Mother...I'm a married woman with a home of my own and I don't think Daddy would approve of this...and in spite of Daddy, I think maybe it'd just be better for everybody if I just packed up and went home...my home is in Iowa now, though I guess I had to come here where I used to live to realize that...*if* you'll excuse me..."

She turned contemptuously from her mother and put a foot on the stairs to mount at last to her room; let her damned mother stew in her own—

—The sudden lance of pain in her right buttock caused her to cry out with a whinnying, adolescent's shriek of fear and surprise: "*Yaaaahhh!*" She turned, tripped and sat backwards on a stair, clutching the bannister for support and for a moment her eyes were level with Wyn's, whose hand was still lifted, fingers curved talon-like from the savage pinch she'd just given her daughter, her eyes burning damply in a rage-mottled face: *"Mature!"* she crowed. "Mature, my eye! I'll have no more of this in my house, believe you me! Now you just *scoot*, you scoot right on up those stairs, only child, and don't you set foot out of your room until you're ready to apologize. Now scoot! You hear me? *Scoot!*"

The front door decisively slammed, freezing them into their positions. Vernon Noel's cheerful voice floated in to them: "Hi, everybody! I'm home!"

FIFTEEN

Miller Springstead sat on the green corduroy sofa in the living room; the Steyr pistol lay to one side, but he didn't feel like any more target practice on the dead mouse tacked to the chunk of firewood in the fireplace.

Anyhow, he hadn't come close yet—and one of the steel-jacketed military rounds had gone all the way through the wood and made a big divot in the mortar lining the back of the fireplace. He'd recovered the slug, not at all badly misshapen, and had been rolling it around on his palm.

Across his bare knees wrapped in an old green flannel shirt was the Japanese officer's sword Turner'd brought back from the war. Once Miller'd asked him if it was the one he'd used to kill that Jap lieutenant on Betio; Turner'd looked at him sourly: "I'm sorry as hell I ever mentioned that shit. Telling war yarn's a stupid and sad-ass fucking thing to do. No, it ain't—I traded a guy an Arisaka I had for it, and I don't know why I did it. Or why I had the damn Arisaka in the first place. Or if I do I ain't saying. Do me a favor, no more about that old shit, now, that's all in the past, okay?"

On the cushion beside him was the bottom drawer from Turner's old chest of drawers and the things that'd been in the drawer. The bottom of the empty drawer was neatly lined with a yellowing front page from the August 7, 1947 *Detroit News*. When they'd moved to Iowa, Miller had left the stuff in this particular drawer—the others contained mostly Turner's collection of wool socks and various blankets and sheets—right in the chest and hadn't really touched anything in it save the pistol which he took out occasionally, unloaded, oiled, reloaded, and put back. On the cushion beside him was the holster for the Steyer, a foot-long Muskie lure Turner'd made with dorsal, pectoral and ventral fins cut from sheet metal, a nearly full box of the archaic and now almost unobtainable Steyr military ammo; and a five by eight envelope full of photos, mostly of poor snapshot quality, that Turner'd brought back from the war—mostly GIs in grinning groups or pairs, photos of various kinds of artillery pieces on which more GIs—grinning! always grinning—slouched or lay or clung, their young faces split by optimistic grins that projected a kind of joyous pride, as if they recognized they were caught up in the biggest experience of their lives. They showed little concern for the rubble and engines of war about them as they were photographed against downed and shell-perforated fighter planes that bore the rising sun on their abdomens, or before huge artillery pieces with names painted on the barrels like BANZAI BUSTER or ABLE ARROW. And among them Turner appeared from time to time. Miller held a finger and blocked the bottom half of one photo of Turner: his eyes, forehead, even hairline, though the hair was dark and thick even with its crew cut, might have been Miller's. Without the finger, though, you saw Turner's aggressively square chin, and an almost brutal Tatar's jaw in contrast to Miller's more pointed one. And the mouth was not thin like Miller's, but full, half-open and loose, bespeaking humor, strength.

Another photo Miller'd just examined had fallen to the floor: a Jap corpse sprawled in the mud on its back, legs crumpled beneath, bare torso thrust upward as though to perform a bench press. The limbs looked inflated and smooth.

Slowly Miller unwrapped the sword from the tattered green flannel. It had a hard-leather sheath and a carved handle wrapped with some kind of laquered twine. Blue and dark brown cords with tassles at the end passed through the hole in its hilt. He pressed the release catch and the blade slid out about a foot seemingly of its own accord, the gleaming metal filmed with pleasantly scented gun oil. Miller pressed his index finger against the naked edge of the blade.

He drew it back: a thin red line traversed it, and when he held the finger before his eyes so the cut faced downward, the red line coalesced into a drop of blood perfect in its shape as a pearl.

SIXTEEN

"...you know you can be a little willful, too, sweetheart," Lindsay's father was telling her. "But I guess I'm just as surprised as you that your mother'd actually *strike* you...want me to get you a drink?" They sat side-by-side on the GI-taut candy-striped spread on Lindsay's bed (made so precisely by Hilary), their shoulders touching, their heads bent; Lindsay'd told her father she wasn't going to leave this room (except maybe to go to the bathroom) until she left for good: she was going to the Hills to stay tonight, and she was getting flights as early as possible to fly back to Iowa City tomorrow. They found themselves whispering though the door was shut.

"No, thanks. I didn't mean it, exactly, what she did was, and this was worse than when she slapped me, when I started up the stairs she came up behind me all pissed off and pinched me, oh it hurt, hooked her damn fingers into me right *here*!"—she slapped herself smartly on the rump—"on the *fanny!*"

"Well, yes. I see." He started to grin, but checked himself: "Good thing you had jeans on—for once, huh? But you must admit you can be pretty provoking yourself, sweetheart. Which is not to excuse *her*, of course. But Wyn's dead wrong in this case—pinching her twenty-three year-old daughter..."

Now Lindsay could not repress a grin herself, and as soon as her father saw it, he smiled widely: "That's the spirit. We Noels have to stick together—you and me, that is."

"That's what Miller'd say, only about the Springsteads, meaning him and me...and you know, I didn't think of myself as a Springstead at all at the time, but now I think maybe I do...that's sort of why I have to go back tomorrow, Daddy, it's not really Mom or anything like that...really. And I need to get back right away, I don't want to be like the stupid Lady Bug that didn't fly away home in time...you see why I have to go, don't you?"

Her father seemed to sag a little more with each of her sentences. He leaned forward with a resigned sigh to flick an

174

imaginary speck of dust from one of his wingtips, then muttered a grudging Yeah.

*

As he drove Lindsay to the Hills where she'd spend the night—Milton'd said he'd be happy to take her over to Traverse in the morning to catch the 7:10 plane to Chicago, where she'd have a three hour layover and if everything went right get to Cedar Rapids, Iowa, around 3:30 in the afternoon—her father's unhappiness was easy to read: as sunlight whisked in yellow waves across his sunglassed eyes, she could see they were crimped around the edges and his whole face bespoke pain; since he'd lost so much weight, his grins were like winces.

Lindsay looked out the window as the Olds whispered through the lovely evening. The nearly full moon hung in the western sky like a spectral medallion, and she wondered again about Miller: where he was, exactly, and what doing.

They made their goodbyes in the parking lot not far from the Lodge's front doors. She tried to make him feel better: "Daddy, I feel so *awful* leaving now after I've just got here, practically, but I've just got to get back and make sure everything's okay, Miller and I'll figure it out together, you'll see, and we'll be back for...oh, Thanksgiving or something..."

"Sure." His lower lip stuck out like a child's who'd been denied candy, and she yearned to fling her arms around him, this lovely foolish human teddy bear: she could never do anything so awful he wouldn't welcome her back with open arms...no matter what..."

"...so can you use a little money?" he was asking, reaching inside his suit coat pocket, extracting from his billfold an already-written check and half a dozen fifty dollar bills." Here, honey, I want you to take this to tide you over...for mad money, huh?"

"Okay..." She wasn't up to resisting just now. She put the check and bills loose into her purse; she'd put them in her billfold later.

"Well," he said huskily, his eyes beginning to glisten with tears.

"Yes. Well..."

"Honey—"

"—Daddy, it's *okay*, now don't even bother getting out of the car, I'll get my bag, it's not even heavy...guess all along I wasn't planning on staying long..."

He hugged her to him; his lips were warm against the cheek that still tingled from Wyn's slap, and she let herself linger against his soft comforting bulk for a few seconds, then forced herself away.

She got outside quickly with her suitcase. "Bye, Daddy. I love you, I'll be in touch."

"You tell Milt I'll call him tomorrow...you take care, now, you're the basket I have all my eggs in..."

Goodbye, goodbye...she walked through the doors and toward the desk. She saw Milton waiting for her, militarily erect in his white ducks, Topsiders and blue blazer. He waved. She remembered when she used to wear this same costume to be cute when they came to dinner at the Hills and what a kick Milton used to get out of it. It suddenly seemed like it'd been a long time since she'd had that kind of silly fun.

*

"Uh-huh, uh-huh, uh-huh," she found herself murmuring in assent to what Milton was saying to her across the sparkling white tablecloth.

"Now of course you can't foretell what it all means for the economy, but something in me trusts LBJ, he's a clever one...though maybe Goldwater, misguided as he is, had the right idea that we should've just bombed the bejesus out of them until they were back in the stone age. But of course..."

Uh-huh, uh-huh... Lindsay really wasn't listening to him, but thinking of how it had been years ago in Bay City: it seemed then that if there was anything her father couldn't take care of, then Milton could: toys, devices, burns, cuts, hurt feelings, anything. She'd never known Milton when he was young—when she was ten, he was already nearly sixty. But now there seemed a new kind of oldness about him, as if his essential spryness had diminished; he seemed more veinous now, almost trembly, his skin made you think of a book-pressed leaf. "Uh-huh, sure, Uncle Milton, that makes sense to me...but we really didn't see all that much protest at Iowa...there's a place on campus called the Pentacrest where there's a silent vigil every Friday afternoon...but they just stand

176

around together kind of meditating for half an hour or so and then they leave..."

Milton's University of Michigan ring still twinkled merrily in the candlelight and his dress was as idiosyncratically natty as ever. But his dewlaps were like something dried on his skin, and his skull, easily visible beneath his thinning whorls of bright white hair, was pink as a baby's.

"...and my people are getting after me to delegate more and more of my authority, but...you know how Doug MacArthur put it in his farewell speech, Old soldiers never die, they just fade away? Well, hogwash! I say you get on top and stay there every last day until one morning instead of you combing your hair, the undertaker does it for you. You take away a man's work and unless he's got a family to melt back into, what is he? A damn husk, occupying space, that's about all I got to say about it.." He seemed more querulous than authoritative, though, and Lindsay wondered where Miller was, at this moment: she saw him outside in Iowa City, meditatively grilling a hamburger on their Arkla gas grill, then settling back on their plastic and aluminum beach chair to eat and have a beer and watch the moon. And think about her and wonder where she was at this moment, she hoped.

"...and then Vern's attack made us both a little jumpy, I guess, I tell you, Lindsay, if I ever do retire, it'll be to Arizona, which is I believe the healthiest of climes..."

The word *attack* startled her to attention. Milton had not been watching Lindsay as he rambled; a rim of congealing tomato juice he'd already have napkin'd away had it been a year ago clung to his upper lip, and he was watching one of his waitresses across the room waiting on a table of young businessmen; she was flirtatiously kidding with them. He scowled.

"Uncle Milton—what did you mean, attack? What attack did Daddy have?"

He thought for a moment, then answered evasively: "Why, I just meant...Vern had, uh, to tone down his high-living a bit, you know, change his diet and things like that..."

"Uncle Milton: tell me. What attack?"

"Well, I...damnit now, you weren't to know, me and my big mouth..."

"Uncle Milton..."

"Well, Vern had a slight—what they call a *minor*—heart

177

attack, a very brief coronary occlusion. He was in the hospital for about a week, and he did just fine. It was in February and he knew you were having a tough time out there in Ioway and didn't want to put any additional strain on you." He displayed the pink slightly wrinkled underside of his hands to her. "I wasn't trying to put one over on you, honest, Linny, but I promised your father, that was how Vern wanted it. I hope you won't tell him I spilled the beans..." A rheum of sincerity glazed his eyes.

"Well, sure, uh-huh I guess but..." He hadn't the *right* she was thinking: how dare he? She could have flown to his side in hours, she could have gotten away from beastly February in Iowa with its incredible dullness, grayness, the penetrating chill, maybe the time away would have been her and Miller's salvation. In any event, it might have given her a sense of *purpose*. And usefulness.

"Look, honey, I've got to get back in the kitchen for a moment, okay? I'm going to tell Thelma to pull Sharon back into line—I'm damned if I'm going to let her carry on like that. My God, you give some of these locals a job where they can make a little scratch and...well, never mind, I won't be long, okay? Your order'll be along toot sweet, the new chef's a lot faster than Raoul ever was, Henry his name is, better get started on your salad..."

She took Milton's advice and rather mechancially started on her salad, thinking of what her mother had said when she told them last August she and Miller were going to get married: *Yes, now you are finally taken care of! Yes! Yes! Go marry your junkman's son and raise a snotty little tribe of greasemonkies and be damned! See how you like living in a grubby little hole in the wall and doing out your undies in the sink every night! See how you like it! Just see!*

Then her father had been at her side, holding her by elbow and upper arm: "Lindsay, honey, it's not that your mother and I ever remotely wanted to choose your man, even less that we object to a good, well-educated local man...I mean this is God's country and never once have I regretted leaving Bay City and setting up shop in the North. But the Springstead boy, and I like him just fine, he's polite and respectful and speaks well, but he comes from stock so country you can call it hillbilly, I...well, it just has all taken me a bit aback, it's like when I was in my early 20s and I caught a glimpse of my bald spot in the mirror for the first time..." But then, Vernon asked two questions in rapid sucession: "Do you love him?"

(She nodded affirmatively, briskly.) You aren't pregnant, are you?" (She pressed her lips together as she had done when as a child when she got so mad she couldn't talk—he got the idea.)

"Well, then," Vernon had said with a short laugh like a bark. He said to Wyn: "Looks like we raised a daughter with a mind of her own and what they commonly call spunk. I say it's time for a drink. What'll we have? A Daquiri? Nah, too lady-like. A Cuban Libre...I got it: let's try a Zombie, I never made one before, so this should be a challenge..."

There came Milton, back from the kitchen, face ruddy with righteousness. And behind him she could see a waitress bearing their orders.

SEVENTEEN

Miller jerked bolt upright on the chair before his desk and one his arms convulsively swept a coffee cup to the floor—but instead of bouncing harmlessly on the carpeting it landed on a quarter full bottle of Jim Beam resting on its side and broke into fragments with a sound like a lightbulb dropped on a sidewalk. The sound plucked Miller to his feet as though he'd been jerked by a string. His eyes were still shut and his fists clenched, but nothing could prevent his memory from bringing back Lindsay's confession of the day before yesterday: Christ, he thought, you try to keep a grip on things and concentrate on keeping things whole and maintaining forward movement rather than stumbling into a downhill slide and you keep at it until the deaths of Rex and Turner become part of everyday life the way an electric hum becomes part of your life if you work in an office, and then Lindsay comes along and tells me Yes, my suspicions are not unfounded, that she really did go and fuck Randy Wilder— another of those smooth monied pricks who've always been my nemesis, from Harlan Flanders to the tall drink of water with the little blond that time at the U of M. They followed me even here to the hinterlands of Iowa. It was just night before last though it seems both minutes and years ago at the same time. This note, I said, explain to me this note I found lying on the bedroom floor from Randy (whom I'd briefly met at the Colonial where he worked part-time, a prick at the Writers' Workshop who knew Lindsay from her U of M days and who used to date her after she broke up with the love of her life before me): *Dearest Lyn, Unforseen exigency prevents our meeting. Call, I love you, Rand.* Have I not been bedeviled by these slick suave monied bullshit artists all my days?

It was about five in the morning, Lindsay having gotten back from the second shift at the Colonial around four- thirty. I'd been up reading *Lear*, which I was teaching in my Core Lit class. So Lindsay and I smoked some Columbian weed she'd gotten from

180

the prick in question. I'd known the instant after she'd offered her explanation—"Oh, it's just Randy's mode of expression, that's just kind of how he talks, it doesn't mean anything, Miller, *honest...*"—that she was lying.

She'd already told me she thought she'd have to go home for a little while: to think and to "just get away from Iowa for a little while."

"Home, eh?" I needled her. "I thought that's where are you are now. I mean, till death us do part? In sickness and in health and all that?"

"Damn you, Miller, I was just feeling half-way decent for the first time in weeks and you're spoiling it...my high, I mean..."

"Sorry, I sympathize with you, I do." I wore only gym shorts and Lindsay had a robe on over her underwear. I dug my toes into the nap of the rug. "Here all life seems to be is just your working your pretty buns to a frazzle for a pittance which we then spend for water and gas and electricity and food and grass and booze and insurance and stuff like that—meanwhile your old man in Michigan mocks me because just out of his petty cash coffers he could supply us with anything we might need. Speaking of quaking bogs, y'ever hear that that's the only place your herb Rosemary'll grow? On quaking bogs? They used to sprinkle it on graves in Elizabethan times, like in *Hamlet* when Ophelia dies...what's the matter?"

"Nothing." I watched a tear like a sticky pearl roll down her cheek.

"Whoops! Goddamnit all!" I'd been fiddling with our dope pipe and had unscrewed it so some of the weed we kept stored inside spilled out on the rug. I began to pick it up piece by piece and replace it.

"Miller..."

"Mmmmm?"

"I...you were right all along. It did happen. With Randy and me, I did what you said, I went right ahead I just did..."

"I know," I said, feeling I knew nothing at all about anything except that I was dead somewhere inside and was bound to get deader with each word she further spoke.

"...and it wasn't that I loved him or anything, it was just somehow I was sick and tired and sad and lonely and tired out and I don't know maybe I was just horny or something like anybody else and maybe because...oh, maybe just to have someone really *prize* me and think maybe I was something that should be cherished...and...I can't *help* it because I didn't grow up in a chicken coop or a coal bin, you go around belittling me and my parents...maybe I just wanted some real affection instead of having it like it's got lately where you come to me either because you think I want you to or you should or because you're horny but not because you love me and want me at the same time like before and after we were first married..." Tears were running freely down both cheeks now.

And so did I go to her and say: I have been a miserable sonofabitch, I will absorb this as punishment, for I love you and you are more sinned against than sinning in this relationship, and we will pull these pieces together, oh listen, baby, let's go back, let's go back to Michigan and let us find some reasonable way to live in Ermine Falls, this professor business has all been madness, let's with some kind of good will and honesty and love see what we can salvage out of these shards lying about us, shall we?

No. I fitted the two pieces of the pipe back together and said, "There." I hefted it. "Good as new." The untethered screen door blew open once with a gust and slammed back hard enough to latch itself. Outside, a whisper of rain was mounting to a hiss. "Almost," I said.

The door rattled fretfully and damp gusts whistled into the living room. And suddenly I was on my feet, bounding past her, hitting the aluminum door with my shoulder so it slammed back against the house with a sound like a pistol shot.

In moments I found myself clinging to the base of the Dutch elm on the median between Center Avenue and the sidewalk in front of our house as the waves of blown rain swept over me.

I looked back to see Lindsay on the porch, holding onto the little metal balustrade. She was drenched in moments, her thin robe clinging to her like a wet sheet. As I watched, she gathered the sodden folds around her hips and ran awkwardly down the steps toward me—at which moment a jagged serpent's tongue of pure white lightning burst nearby and with hardly any lag thunder rolled and resounded tumultously around us in damp waves of tactile sound. The acrid scent of ozone tainted the air. She stumbled against me, then, for protection; then she stepped away a pace so she could peer into my face.

182

"Bastard was close," I said, "wonder it didn't lay us out like a couple of pole-axed steers. Or like Paolo and Francesca in *The Inferno*, done in with a single sword stroke. No such luck for us, I guess, huh?"

There didn't seem to be any more lightning in the vicinity, and you could already see the beginnings of false dawn in the east where the sky was becoming tinged with the blue of venous blood as it rushes home to the heart for oxygen.

"Why's that X on the tree?" she asked in a small voice I could barely hear over the sound of wind and water.

I looked at the flourescent Day-Glo X spray-painted on the side of the tree. "Means this bugger's got Dutch Elm Disease and the city'll be along one of these days to cut her down."

"Oh no."

"Oh yes."

Leaving me, she ran toward the house.

*

It was three in the morning. And once again Miller Springstead could hear a ringing in the house, not of emptiness but of something else he couldn't identify. He went into the living room and fell back on the sofa. Idly he laid the Japanese sword across his legs.

So this is what it all comes down to, he thought. Rex gone, Turner gone, Lindsay gone. Once I thought I could pull out of the gloom the death of my family had cast me into like The Little Engine That Could—with Lindsay by my side and a new place to go into and goals to aim for, all that would lift me like some aircraft whose faltering engine suddenly caught again and came to full power and pulled up out of a long dangerous dive verging on a tailspin.

It was time for a drink, then maybe he could if not sleep then drowse off for a while into some wooly place that wasn't here.

EIGHTEEN

She awoke with a start, and though she didn't at first recognize where she was, she looked to the bedside table where she always kept her alarm. The clock said three, and she was at first befuddled enough to have to figure out it must be three a.m. because she could see part of the moon out her window.

Oh, yes: here she was at the Hills, trying to get rested up for the flights in the morning: to Chicago, then on to Cedar Rapids, where she'd rent a car or take a taxi or something to get home. Home. God.

Dirty lumps of moonlight spilled through the curtains and fell across her legs. She was sweating, tense. She had been dreaming of Miller, Miller last fall, after their first terrible fight in October and he gone cursing off into the night on foot and had later come home smashed. She had wakened at three and gone to the door, thinking she'd heard something. Peeping through the slats of the venetian blinds, she watched him coming along Center Avenue, drenched in the platinum light of a quarter moon. His shoulders were white with the moonlight, as though he'd been dusted with salt or stone dust. He was walking slowly, and there was something decrepit about his movements, which were usually graceful and fluid. He carried a can of beer in one hand.

What happened next was almost slapstick: adjusting his stride to apparently give it a freewheeling and jaunty aspect (in case, she supposed him thinking, anyone might be watching, like his wife), Miller suddenly slipped to his knees on the sidewalk. And then, instead of getting up, he continued to walk on his kneecaps as though they were stumps. With each truncated step he seemed to try and then fail to gather enough strength to regain his feet. And so he waddled grotesquely forward, all the while holding the single can foolishly in front of him as though it was a precious and irrecoverable antidote to something.

Just suppose, she thought to herself, twisting on the sheets on her bed in her room at the Hills. Just suppose. S'pose we hadn't fallen into this myth where Miller had to strive upward to bridge the gap between junkyard and profdom. S'pose we'd both just chosen to stay where we were. Where he was. Where he'd grown up. S'pose instead of rejecting the junkyard, we'd both *chosen* it, *embraced* it, given up those other laughable pretensions and lived as Thorcau'd said he'd wanted to live when he went to the woods: deliberately, and s'pose we'd had us a garden and some chickens and maybe a cow and gone fishing when we felt like it and looked for Morrell mushrooms in the spring and then picked apples in the fall from the wild crazy Springstead orchard up behind their place where Miller told me they buried their animals, we could've had cats and dogs and maybe a horse and Miller would come in sweaty from hard work in the yard and I'd've baked bread and while it cooled he'd clean up and we'd make love and have a big salad from our own garden and then the bread would be cool enough to cut easily...later we'd sit on the porch holding hands on a creaking swing and watch the fireflies and the moon could never be a malevolant reminder of something or other but instead always a brotherly presence for both of us...suppose, suppose...

But maybe that too was just another delusional projection, an absurd half-assed (as Miller would say) romantic vision half-born of half-reading Emerson and Thoreau in American Lit: and in trying to make the projection real she'd only have ended up as Madame Bovary in Dogpatch, not a noble spirit hand-in-hand with her chosen mate.

But suppose: anyway, just suppose...

NINETEEN

The plane was somewhere between Chicago and Cedar Rapids, and half in a drowse, with her head pressed against the little window (she always asked for No Smoking window seats, though there was a certain disadvantage if you had to go to the bathroom), she groggily tried to formulate a sincere apology to her mother (in spite of it all): Mom, really I am sorry; I'm sorry you didn't get what you wanted (though I now have the sinking feeling nobody does), at least from me, and I know how you wanted it to be: Royal and I come home for Christmas from Grosse Point or Bloomfield Hills or wherever and we meet you and Daddy at the door all bundled up in our ski togs (for it is snowing great picturesque flakes) and laden with stacks of gaily wrapped and ribboned packages...Royal is a little drunk as are you, you and he have come to like one another and you get along swimmingly. You usher us inside where by the snapping fire there are sandwiches (with the crusts cut off like I used to like them as a little girl) and hot cocoa so thick it's like drinking a chocolate bar and a pitcher of some kind of toddies and the air is alive with the bright piney tang of Christmas—"Come in, come *in*," you urge us, and later when we are all seated at the dining room table, you and Daddy and Milton and Royal and I, all of us a little bloated from the sumptuousness Hilary or whoever's prepared, Daddy and Milton and Royal are about the finish their Drambouies and repair to the den, you and I, Mom, will continue to sip at our champagne as we chat, mother and daughter, about the prices of everything, the degeneration of the good and genteel in life, the elevation of the shabby, what's happening with any mutual acquaintances, perhaps we will even get into recipes, perhaps Jerry and Evonne Puckett are coming by later, you look at me and smile and your hand, soft as doeskin, delicately veined, comes out on the sparkling tablecoth and you squeeze my hand and murmur, "Oh, Lindsay, I'm so glad everything's turned out so well after all..." "Yes," I say, "yes, Mom, me too," as the champagne in those hollow-stemmed goblets from your own wedding over a

186

quarter of a century ago effervesces into the Christmassy air...

Crap. All crap. Lindsay opened her eyes and watched ragged sheets of vapor whip past the window as the plane sped toward Cedar Rapids some twenty or so minutes distant. There was some rain, too, though she recalled the captain over the speaker saying the weather was clear in Cedar Rapids. As she kept peering through the window, the gray did lighten from leaden to a dull blue, and red, orange and vermillion began to stain the eastern-most horizon.

*

Minutes after the aircraft touched down, she plunged into a swamp-moist Iowa afternoon—it felt like ninety in the shade and the air almost seared your lungs.

Lindsay was sweating lightly into a large blue oxford-cloth shirt of her father's that she had appropriated for the trip and wore with the tails flapping around a pair of white Levi's; she could already feel her face dampen with that Iowa film of oily sweat. But she walked toward the small airport purposefully, almost proudly, somehow cheered and feeling cooly adequate to almost any situation.

First things first: she'd go see if Miller'd come to get the Volvo, since she had a spare key in her billfold. If he had already taken it, then she'd just get a Hertz car; she wouldn't even bother with a cab or airport limousine or bus.

Maybe if the Volvo weren't there she'd go to the bar and call Miller and maybe it'd be kind of cute if she'd get a little drunk waiting for him to come get her.

She could explain to him how on the plane between Traverse City and Chicago she had recalled something from her physical science course (who said education wasn't good for something, huh?) that she'd taken at Michigan and which she'd only by the skin of her teeth gotten a B in. It had been a kind of dumb course, just watered down physics, really, and math and some philosophical baloney, yet one piece of it stuck in her mind, the law of the conservation of energy, of which her text, *Vitalized Physics*, told her: "Energy is never created and never destroyed; the total amount in the universe is constant, and all that ever happens to it is that it changes its form..." Is that right? she'd ask Miller. And what about your energy and my energy, is that the same kind of deal, and if it is, what does it all mean? And in the course of things he could explain for her as he'd promised but never done what The Second Law of Thermodynamics and the thing called Entropy was all about...

She was getting closer to where she'd left the Volvo— and sure enough, there it sat, glowing dully through its film of dust. The afternoon sun had emerged from the clouds, and it glinted off parked cars making Lindsay feel good. But then her slap-happy confidence turned to a cube of ice: the strap of her leather purse that she'd carried for the past three years, that she took everywhere, that Daddy got her in Acapulco, was no longer looped around her left arm.

No, she'd had it when she got off the plane, hadn't she? Did that mean that after all her travelling about, she'd had her goddamn pocket picked, so to speak, in Cedar Rapids, Iowa?

My purse, my billfold, my handful of fifty dollar bills, Daddy's check, my driver's license, my American Express card, my housekey, Volvo key, my pictures of Daddy and Milton by the plane, a photo of Miller, grinning, standing outside our house—she thrust a hand into her white Levi's. She didn't even have a dime to make a phone call.

She could feel a rueful grin turn her lips down at the corners: I'll get the police, she thought, they can't do this to me! I'm Lindsay Noel. Lindsay Noel Springstead.

TWENTY

From behind a portly businessman smelling powerfully of cigar and gin who was picking up the Hertz car he had reserved, Lindsay watched the girl in her perky uniform getting the keys, the papers, trying to sell the man some insurance. Lindsay found something about her compelling.

"Yes, miss?" The cigar-scented man had moved on, pocketing his keys and papers.

Then Lindsay made the connection: like herself the girl was tall and her bare arms smoothly muscled, though her hair — shoulder-length rather like her own—was dull blonde rather than russet or, as Daddy liked to say, auburn. Like Lindsay's, the girl's face was even-featured with a small nose: We might almost be twins, Lindsay thought with a sense of wonder. Except of course that she wore no makeup at all while her double wore plenty; but even the mascara and almost garish eye shadow swallowtails at the far corners of the girl's hazel eyes did not disguise the resemblance: We could almost be before-and-after for Maybelline or Revlon, Lindsay thought. What a pretty girl—and what nice teeth. Maybe a little nicer than mine.

And this girl (LIN COLLINS said the nameplate on her Hertz blazer) looked happy: her skin, smile, hair, lips, small-diamonded engagement ring all said so.

"Miss?" Lin Collins looked strangely at Lindsay: was she too perceiving the resemblance, or did Lindsay just look a little spaced-out or something? But it'd been a while since she'd had two Screwdrivers on the flight from Traverse City (so I must have had my purse *then*, I paid a dollar for each of the drinks...).

"Look," Lindsay said, turning her empty palms upward before Lin Collins, "I need some help—some assistance."

"How can I help?"

"I've lost my purse—actually, I think somebody lifted it on the plane or at the airport...and I just got here and my car's in the parking lot locked and all I've got is my suitcase—or I'll have it as

189

soon as I go get it from baggage, at least I still have my claim
ticket—and all I have in it is my clothes and stuff. Who do I go see?
What do I do? My husband's in Iowa City—I've just got to get back
there right away, it could even be a matter of life and death!"

There were no other customers. Lin Collins tapped the metal
band of her pencil against her beautiful front teeth so it made an
audible *toc-toc-toc*.

"Well," she said finally, "I don't know what *I personally* can
do...but, the Traveller's Aid person"—she looked beyond Lindsay's
shoulder to verify—"went to lunch a while back, but they'll be back
after while. Right now maybe you should go check with your
airline—you flew in on United from Chicago? And you...maybe you
can put a tracer on your bag, or get some advice from them, or
maybe you need a policeman..."

"Look, I need a car right now is what I need. I just can't wait,
I've got to get back...can't you cut your red tape or something? I
have—*had*—an American Express card in my purse...*I know*: you
can call my father in Michigan and *he'll* vouch for me and you can
put the car on *his* American Express, there, how's that?"

"Miss, even so I couldn't give you a car without a valid driver's
license..."

"For God's sake, who'd have an invalid one?" Lindsay snapped.
"I have a perfectly good Michigan driver's license, I just don't have
it *with* me, Daddy could probably vouch for that too if you'd just
give him a ring..."

"Miss...I'm sorry about what's happened, but we'd still need
some kind of documentation from you, even if we reached your
father and charged a car to his account. Do you have any identifi-
cation in your suitcase, or your pockets or something?"

"No...no, I don't...God. It's like without those goddamn little
scraps or paper and plastic I don't exist. Not to mention I had six
fifty dollar bills that that son of a bitch, whoever it was, stole too!
But right now I've got to get to Iowa City. Like soon!"

"Look," Lin Collins, rising color betraying a certain exaspera-
tion, "I don't really think I'm the one to help you: you can wait for
the Traveller's Aid people or you can check with with your airline.
Call the police...or maybe what would be best would be to call one
of your friends or your husband or whoever in Iowa City and have
them come get you..look, here, I'll give you a dime, compliments of
Hertz, and there's a pay phone over there. You see? And while

you're waiting for them to get here you can at least report your loss at the United counter and maybe get some further advice from them...okay?"

A bulky woman who'd appeared a few moments earlier and had been standing behind Lindsay shifted impatiently and when Lindsay stepped aside, she set her tote bag with some relief on the counter in front of Lin Collins.

*

I paused in the steamy interior of the phone booth, trying to decide what to do. Should I call Miller...or just take a taxi and hope that when he got me home Miller'd be there and could pay him? Or who could I ask for money to take a bus or something? I brought the dime close to my face and sniffed, it was filmed with my sweat and smelled like guns.

I looked from the booth over to the Hertz counter: Lin Collins was no longer there and in her place was a short, dark-haired girl with a pixie haircut and huge round glasses.

That was when I knew I couldn't call Miller. What if he wasn't sober? But it wasn't that so much as that I was determined to see this through all on my own, this one time I would not stamp my feet and yell and pout and then hightail it for Ann Arbor, this time I would seize the wretched boy's goddamn penis and give it a tremendous yank! I would rip off and fling my blood-sodden underpants in their leering simpleton faces, and to Miller I would cry out in what he assured me was bad Shelley, *I fall on the thorns of life! I bleed!*

And I would get back to Miller, back to our home, under my own power and appear to him firm and resolute if haggard, self-sufficient, self-reliant, maybe even brave...

At which point it occurred to me that the only person, queerly enough, that I felt I could really trust at the moment was the person I'd betrayed Miller with, Randy Wilder!

My slippery fingers dropped the dime into the phone.

TWENTY-ONE

Randy'd weathered things in her absence all right, in fact he looked splendid, his dark-gold hair lustrous and cut a little shorter than usual, his skin shining with health. For a moment she almost hated his spruceness for its contrast against what she felt was her own bedraggled state.

Randy Wilder's snappy red Fiat convertible snored along comfortably and she kept her eyes on him. Their greeting had been almost formal—he had given her a brief peck on the cheek like some adolescent greeting his prom date before her parents. Now that she had begun listening to what he was saying, she was beginning to discern that his high spirits had something to do with some kind of success he had in the Writers' Workshop where he had finished his MFA last January (but was ostensibly hanging around waiting for her to leave Miller and cast her lot with him); in fact she was beginning to suspect that this "success" had emboldened him to make that ill-advised and totally indiscreet call he'd made to Ermine Falls that Wyn'd intercepted. "I mean, God," he was saying, "it was like just incredible, I mean what a bitch—except for you, for us, of course—this last year's been, I mean for the longest time I couldn't write a decent poem to save my soul, I thought maybe I'd already run dry while I was still unpublished. But you remember how after we got reacquainted and I sort of fell for you all over again and Royal wasn't there beating my time, then I started writing all those love poems?"

"When it rains it pours, huh?"

"Yeah, something like that...but, you see, what's got me on this upper is...see, I needed some good acceptances to go with my MFA before I try to get some soft touch of a teaching job someplace. And all of a sudden *three* came through for me, two of them in the same mail...isn't that something?"

"Three acceptances for what?"

"Acceptances for my work! My poems!" He smacked the steering wheel jubilantly with one hand. "The day you left, *Road Apple Review* came through for me. Then the next day, this new mag, *Primary Sources* in British Columbia, and *Poetry Northeast*, they each took a poem. They were pretty long poems too. The one in *Road Apple Review* is a love poem I call 'Oxymoron,' and it's for you and how bleak February was and then we...sort of discovered, or re-discovered, each other...here are the last lines : 'I discovered during the deeps of that winter/ Smooth and harsh, sweet/ And bitter,/ That this nettle-itch of her/ Is just what I can bear.' Not bad, huh? What I meant to suggest with 'nettle itch of her is just what I can bear' is that kind of ambivalence I feel about you, or did then...how do you like it?"

"Charming. It's a thrill to be called an itch somebody can stand...better than a scratch, I suppose."

A look of irritation flickered then disappeared on Randy's handsome face: "I'm sorry," he said, "I know how it is to be around somebody who's up when you're a bit down—you are, aren't you? Was Michigan a bummer? I love northern Michigan myself, my God, the skiing, the watersports, what more could you want. Did you tell your folks about us? How about Miller before you left? Did you tell him?"

"Yes..."

"Well, that's damned good. Now maybe we can go into further plans, hell, I don't need to go to work just yet, maybe we could spend this whole coming year in Michigan and I can write more poetry and send it out and build up a backlog of publications, maybe even get a book together, and start sending out my applications to some of the schools around the state...Albion, Alma, Hope, Adrian, Central State, Kalamazoo College, Eastern, Western, places like that, probably neither State or Michigan would touch me yet, even though I was a Hopwood Award winner at Michigan...boy, you didn't get much rest and recuperation in Michigan, did you?"

"It shows that much, huh?"

"Yeah. You look beat. You should have had me with you. Next time you go back, we'll go together—we'll go visit the U of M campus as a couple this time, I bet just walking around campus there'd restore us...like the guy in Hemingway's Two-Hearted River stories, huh? Sorry, but I can't stop jabbering, I am so up: so how's your mom and dad and the Olds business and everything?"

"Fine."

"I love The Shack. I can't believe your old man hardly ever does more than have his pals there for lunch every now and then in the summer. Could we live there? Wouldn't that be something? You

193

and me together while I work on my writing? Christ, baby, what a blast that could be...skiing at Boyne Mountain in the winter...or Ermine Hills when you don't want to drive that far, the slopes there aren't all that nifty, but what the hell..."

"Don't call me baby, would you, I don't like that word."

"Jesus. You're touchy. Well, okay, sure. I'm sorry. I can see you're not too excited about my publications. They don't mean much to you, do they?"

"Sure, of course, I'm happy for you, Randy...like I told you on the phone, you were the only person I could really depend on in Iowa City to help me out of a jam like this...it really means something having somebody you can count on, I...am I haggard? I guess I am. If I'm not I should be. You know, while I was waiting for you I found two dollar bills in the pocket of my father's shirt and that was just enough to have two Bloody Marys in the bar, though I didn't have anything to leave for a tip...I was so frustrated from dealing with that big jerk at the United counter, I think he thought I was smuggling dope in my purse or something. God what a horrid time all the way 'round. I remember Miller said the best kinds of tough experiences were the kind that hardened you but didn't coarsen you, but I doubt I'd know the difference even if he's right..."

"Speaking of your erstwhile other half, I want you to just tell him you're leaving with me and pack a bag quick like a bunny and then get out. If he objects, I'll deal with him..."

Suddenly Lindsay could hardly stand the sound of his voice, and she reached out and quickly switched on the radio. How exactly was she going to put it to Randy: she wasn't going anywhere with him; in fact she didn't really even much like him. But this was the man she'd betrayed Miller with in any event, hadn't she? She turned the volume up to drown out her thoughts and as well as any impulse Randy might have to speak. There was a weather report from Davenport (partly cloudy, humidity 80, temperature 90, intermittent thunder showers in the evening, so what else was new), and she turned the knob; there was a snatch of a Mozart piano concerto, then

> Tall and tan
> The girl from
> Ipanema goes walking...

Lindsay tried to relax against the bucket seat. She closed her eyes. After a time, static distorted the station she'd found and Randy sought another. He hit upon a country music station and would have moved on, but Lindsay quickly reached out and stopped his hand.

Four walls to hear me
Four walls to see
Four walls to hear me
Clo-o-o-sin' in on me...

Beautiful, she thought, there's something so...*appropriate* about this kind of stuff when it's really good...

Out where the bright lights are glowing
You're drawn like a moth to a flame
You laugh while the wine's over-flowing
While I sit and whisper your name...

She didn't stop Randy when he reached out again and changed stations; in fact what he chanced upon was rather nice, a Chopin nocturne she recognized that had always made her think of furry ambidextrous animals cleansing their food in a chill stream on a moonlit night.

She kept her eyes shut, and when Randy tried to take her hand, she pulled away restlessly. She felt sun on her face once and opened her eyes to watch hosts of motes like miniscule worlds be shunted around on air currents in the car.

The ride was becoming soothing, lulling. But, she reminded herself, she needed to get ready now to deal with Miller: she'd make Randy let her off a block away from their house, she would promise to call him later, and she would enter their home, assuming it wasn't locked and Miller away, and let whatever was going to happen, happen...

*

She felt like a swimmer stroking slowly up through honey-thick water as she awoke under Randy's hand on her shoulder, urging her into consciousness. Where was she? She opened her eyes to see her lap full of sunlight pied from a rush of shadows through foliage of the tree under which they were parked. Her heart lurched in her chest as she recognized the Day-Glo X on the Dutch Elm in front of the Springstead house on Center Avenue.

"Lafayette, we are here," Randy said.

He lolled back, hands loosely resting on the Fiat's wheel, one knee drawn up. He looked composed and together, his trim chinos and pearl gray knitted sport shirt combining with his tan to make him look like a whiskey ad. But Lindsay noticed that a mustache of sweat lingered on his upper lip, and that when he drummed on fingers on the rim of the wheel, they seemed to tremble a bit.

She reached groggily for the door handle.

Randy's hand closed over hers and prevented her from opening the door. "I'm going in with you," he said. "You may need some protection."

"Absolutely not!" She ripped her hand off the handle and pushed his hand away. "You listen to me, Randy Wilder, there's not going to be any kind of thing with you and Miller, I will not have it! God, sometimes men make me sick! All of you! I'm going to get out now and I want you to drive off and go on home! I'll call you a little later, I promise I will, but now just go! Go home!"

Randy opened his mouth and spoke, but his words were drowned out by the snarl of a chain saw, half a block down on Center Avenue, where two men were cutting down a condemned Dutch Elm from the Center Avenue median.

Before she could open her mouth Randy was out of the car and around in back, where he began to unhook the elastic, octopus-armed thing that had kept her suitcase battened against the rear deck's luggage bars. She got out and went around to the back. The air seemed almost glutenous with humidity but there was no rain; through breaks in forbidding clouds congealing above them, sun-beams kept fighting through, blotching them and the red car with rushes of light and shadow.

"I don't feel right about this, I think it's a bad idea," Randy said, and for the first time they both turned toward the house, brooding on its raised basement and garage. The sprung aluminum screen door had been wrenched back into its original configuration enough so it could be latched. A glossy starling perched on the eave trough over the front door stared brightly at them.

"Call me, like within an hour from now or I'll be back and

there'll be hell to pay," Randy said, and turned to his car.

Lindsay turned and crossed the sidewalk and walked slowly up the walk to the front door, carrying her light suitcase, which nonetheless felt heavy at the moment. Trembling, she pressed the latch and opened the screened door. The front door was half open and when she gave it a little push it swung fully open. It was dark as a cave within—she could see no lights burning and all the shades were drawn.

"Miller, Miller are you here?" she called into the gloom.

There was the sound of movement from a chair, sofa, something with springs.

"Miller?" she called again, suddenly frightened. What if she was too late, what if he was hurt or dead or dying or something? "Miller? Miller?"

There was a throat-clearing sound, then Miller's voice acknowledged his presence: "I am the bitter name."

Beyond the door, she could hear the chain saw starting up again, this time a bit closer.

TWENTY-TWO

"Yes. The bitter name. Did I mumble?" I tell her cheerfully.

Yes, I have seen Randy down there in his little red cocksman's car. He hasn't left yet, so I expect he's waiting to see if anything happens. How can I disappoint that old bottom-feeder?

"Oh indeed I am the bitter name," I tell her. "Here you are all been to good ole Michigan and come back, my ole Linsay-Food-Cake..."

She is almost without resistance as I pull her close against my chest, all I have on are my sweat pants. I squeeze her tight and her man's shirt blots up some of my sweat. I give her a little twirl and watch her spin over the living room floor, almost fall over the coffee table, and collapse on the sofa. "Didn't anybody ever tell you frowns can freeze in place? C'mon, now, it can't be all that bad. Tell ole uncle Miller, he knows where the bear shit in the buckwheat and that's a fact...oh, careful there, don't you set your lovely little bottom the wrong way on my ole Steyr pistola there...oh, nothin' to worry about, there wasn't no burglars invading our lovely abode to violate it or nothing."

Her eyes focus on the dead mouse tacked to the block of fireplace wood.

"Nothing to fret about. I assure you he's deader'n a smelt'n ain't no threat to you no more, Lindsay...you got'im the first time with your Victor trap, there ain't much fight left in the bugger by this stage in the game...say, your ole eyes're big's saucers, 'spect you better lay on back and rest up, you're lookin' a little peaked. And say, ain't that your boyfriend, ole Randy-Dandy down there looking soulfully up here 'case his lady love's being assaulted or something by the ogre who lives here? The Troll-in-Residence, as it were? Hell, we'd best disabuse him on that account—I'll just go invite that ole bottom-feeder on up for a drink'n a chit-chat, hey?"

"No," she says weakly, barely able to lift herself from the sofa; a bit sweaty, dissheveled, with no make-up and her hair a bit tangled, she has never looked lovelier. "Set back!" I order her.

198

I skip to the doorway, poke my head just out the screen door, where I can see Randy levering his suave ass up out of his itty-bitty convertible like he's finally made the decision to present himself on the Springstead doorstep and see just what the fuck's up. So a little encouragement won't be out of order: "Hey, there," I holler down the incline to him, "ole Randy, c'mon up, we've giving away free turkies! One of 'em's got your name on it!"

I wave, motion him to cross the median, then the sidewalk, then come up the cement stairs to the portal of the Springstead home.

He turns toward me, hesitates, then crosses the median.

I step over by Lindsay, give her a little chuck under the chin, then pluck the bottle of Jim Beam from the coffee table; I have a good slug: "Waaah. That cleans out the old pipes..." The Beam burns to the bottoms of my toes and brings tears to my eyes; for a moment I am dizzy...but when I hear Randy come through the door behind me, I seem to feel my strength and balance and whatever wits I have left by this stage return to me.

I turn to tender some Springstead hospitality to Randy: "Well, come right on *in*," I urge him cordially, and as soon as he's all the way in, I slam the big door behind him hard and it makes a satisfying sound like a shotgun blasting a hole in the ground. "Welcome to the Springsteads', palzie-walzie..."

He backs away from me, hands jerking up like a boxer, but I do not pursue, I grin—I think—and wave my arm magnanimously, then turn and hold both my arms wide, to include them both, as if to welcome them both into my embrace: "Hell, just relax, there, old Randy-Dandy, don't fret, ole Miller he ain't completely lost his marbles...I don't think. *Re*-lax, set your suave ole ass down on our sofa which ole Lindsay with her impec-impec-im*pec*able taste snapped up for a mere six hunnerd. G'wan! I recommend it! Honest injun!"

Damn if ole Randy through some residual protocol or something, me being the host after all, don't accept and sit so he and Lindsay are on opposite ends of the sofa. Even seeing them that close together makes something turn over in my guts and I reckon I'd better have another drink. "Careful, there, sport, don't nudge my piece layin' between you guys around none, it ain't got a hair trigger but I wouldn't fuck with it none if I was you..." Randy sees

199

my cocked Steyr with the safety off there in the middle of the sofa and shrinks from it as if it's red hot. "I was just doin' l'il target practice, you see..."

Lindsay's eyes turn toward the mouse and the bullet-marred block of wood in the fireplace and Randy's eyes follow her gaze, then return at the pistol. He winces, I can see this ain't his dish of tea, he's trying to figure how best to get his ass intact out of here and as well spirit my own true love off along with him, both of them leaving her degenerate husband railing and thrashing about in his madness. "That there was Turner's piece," I supply. "Almost an antique by now, old Austrian nine em-em job, but still good for making orifices in just about anything..."

I must have another drink to keep me going so I pluck up the Beam and as I bring it to my lips I hesitate because Randy twists toward Lindsay on the sofa as if he is going to reach out and take her by the hand and simply lead her away from this squalid scene. I am afraid if I see him actually touch her I'll either burst into tears and fall weeping and puling to the floor or else seize him and kill him.

To forestall either I put the bottle back untasted and skip over to the fabulous Springstead study where once upon a time I read the *Collected Poems of Jones Very* with an eye toward making him the subject of my disseration. "Don't worry," I call back from the doorway of the study, "if I was for some reason to want to terrorize your ass, ole Randy-Dandy, I wouldn't do it with no goddamn gun, thass a chickenshit's approach to things. Nossir, I'd do her with some *real* wherewithal."

From the doorway I look hard at Lindsay who is still haggard and drawn and white as a sheet and sitting there quivering on the sofa.

Well, as Rex and I used to say, fuck'em all but six: and save them for pallbearers.

I clear my throat, spit on the floor, and take up Turner's Jap sword from where it has lain on my scholar's desk. I unhook the catch and slide the blade out of the sheath, long lovely razor-sharp shapely heavy mother.

When I enter the living room with the sword, they move closer to one another on the sofa.

Randy reaches for Lindsay's hand but she shakes it off and suddenly rises to face me and cries out in a thin but determined voice: "Miller Springstead, you just *stop*! this juvenile carrying on! Wouldn't your father and brother be proud of you now? *Stoppit*! Why are you doing this?..." Her lips quiver, and all sweaty and earnest and afraid she is impossibly lovely to me; and so I must somehow find the ability in the midst of the chaos I have created to make a rational answer: "Well, I reckon I have somehow reached the point where I've used up just about all the credit as I had here on earth. I'm in pain from being alone and because I have to own up to things with my brother and father and I guess maybe now I just want somebody to bury my dog and horse with me..." Hmmm, maybe that don't make as much sense as I—

"—Miller, this is all *wrong*, I know things now, how about us getting a cow and all, I mean, listen, I know—"

"—You don't know shit!" I cry as I am unable to keep my gaze away from wonder-struck Randy and imagine him stripped with his body covering that of my lovely Lindsay.

Randy rises and moves next to Lindsay whose beseeching eyes remain on my face. Fuck'em all but six.

"Nuffa this fuckin' around. So now old Randy-Dandy, you Joe College dipshit, you see this here fuckin' sword Turner used to win the war with, ain't she a beauty? Maybe I'll use her to liberate your body from your head...but first, to warm up, as it were..."

I have crouched a little and now use my legs to spring toward the sofa, laughing, the echo of my laughter when I learned of Turner's death: and they split apart on either side of the sofa like frightened Guinea hens: *You farmers*! I hear Sandy Dehner spit at me from the past: "Yee-haa! Die, thou damn-ed whale, thus I yield up my axe to theeeee!"

I bring the sword down like I'm an Elizabethan headsman, drive the bastard like an axe down into the middle of Lindsay Noel's six hundred dollar sofa, rending fabric and wood and springs and some gray batting that extrudes from the thing's insides like puddles of brain, the metal springs bright and sharp when I have severed them—

KA-CHUNG! it goes as I drive that sword again and again into the sofa, cutting through more and more of it, the sword is purposefully and perfectly balanced, it gives the wonderful feel of swinging an axe and now the two parts of the sofa are cut all the way through, though still joined by some fabric and the ends lean in forlornly toward each other.

201

It is time to attend to Randy and I turn to him: "Awright, fucker, let's make like Ima fuckin' lawnmower and your ass is grass!" *Gonna show you how how a taller man can use his reach, give you a few boxing tips,* Harlan Flanders whispers from the pain in the back of my head.

Randy moves away, scuttling around by the fireplace, looking wildly for something to defend himself with, but not noticing the fireplace tools on the hearth that'd suit his purposes just perfect—

Lindsay cries out with surprising volume from the doorway to the study where she has fled, "Oh, Miller, you just *stoppit!* I need to tell you things! You awful dope! I love you and you just *stoppit* this minute! You're ruining everything!"

"I know it. And I love you too," I call gently and look one last time at her before I turn to stalk Randy.

And Randy, the tricky bastard, has edged around to the almost bisected sofa, and I feel a grin starting way down in my toes as I watch him in desperation pick up Turner's ancient Steyr.

So I shake the sword and holler: "Yeah! Fuckin' A! Thass the idea!" as he points the gun at me with both trembling hands, holding it as if it's a water hose. I lower the sword and let it drop to the floor. Then I raise both hands with fingers splayed and reach out toward him and start to totter forward like I'm playing Frankenstein's monster: "Now, old Randy, I think I will just sink my fingers into you anywhere you're soft and get me a piece of you and pull on it 'til it comes off like Grendel's arm, whattayou think of that, hey?"

I move toward him, hands still outstretched, the gun barrel waggles absurdly and goes *ka-boomp!* and knocks me deaf and I watch an ejected cartridge whiz through the smoke and I am seized by a huge dust devil out of nowhere and spun around...and next thing I know I'm sitting on the floor by the broken-down sofa, coughing. It would be laughter if I could make it so, but I can't. I look up to see Lindsay coming to me and behind her Randy and my chest feels like its filling up with warm tar.

I hear the house ringing around me. I want to tell Lindsay that now I know what she meant when she said the house *rings*, and now she bends closer, and I want to laugh and can't, but still it rings, goddamnit, *rings*...

But now it all gets quiet and the quiet makes it peaceful, and that makes me think of the way it was just after Turner'd got back from the war and he was jumpy and noise of almost any kind seemed to spook him and Rex and I learned to be quiet around him without any coaching from Sonney or Pearl and we discovered that for part of each day he liked to be where it was quiet and to listen to the quiet like some'd listen to music and maybe we all learned to do this best together on those Sunday afternoons when we'd lock up the shop and drive in the pickup over to Thayer Lake and rent a fourteen foot rowboat and go fishing for sunfish and perch and bluegills. Thayer Lake was always quiet except for bird calls and the occasional outboards, but even they didn't bother us. Dense green foliage was massed all around the rich muddy shore and we always left a firmly sculpted V in the mud after we pushed off, and maybe a footprint or two from me or Rex, whoever pushed us off. And there we'd be all afternoon with our fishing rods and Turner's tackle box among the lily pads, hearing nothing more than the lap of water and birdcalls and a croak from a frog and an occasional splash from a fish or maybe a muskrat. It was the kind of mucky-bottomed out-of-the-way lake the sports who drove speedboats around Silverfish Lake would avoid. And we'd sit there all afternoon and do nothing more than watch our red and white plastic bobbers until the sun began to fade and the shadows deepened and degree by slow degree it became evening.

Lindsay comes closer now, hovering above me, but she is indistinct, too, like a ghost, though a pretty one with her wet face and lovely tangled hair hanging woefully over her shoulders, and now I enter a bubble of peace as well as quiet and it is one of those post-war Sundays and Rex and Turner and I are anchored not too far out from the shady northeastern bank of Thayer Lake among the lily pads, Rex and I wear bib overalls, our tennis shoes, tied together by their strings, are stowed under our seats, his under the bow, mine under the stern, Turner is in the middle and has his work shoes and socks under the seat he sits on, his feet and ankles are large and boney and startlingly white in the shade, he wears a pair of tattered and grease-stained fatigues and a blue workshirt with the sleeves rolled down since he is self-conscious about his scars and a wide-brimmed straw hat he found in the trunk of a wrecked car he bought at auction: and so we three together listen, listen carefully to all the quiet around us as evening comes on.

TWENTY-THREE

There were sharp pains like knitting needles stabbed into the back of her head and Lindsay sneezed and awoke to find herself sitting in their plush yellow easy chair, twisting involuntarily away from an ammonia ampule a young man with a short black brushcut dressed in white was holding under her nose. His other hand gripped her shoulders and kept her pressed into the enveloping chair.

"There, take it easy, miss, it's okay now—you feeling any better?"

"Oh my God!" She twisted again, to no avail, under the firm but also gentle grip restraining her. "Where's my husband—where's Miller?"

"Easy, easy now, the injured party's your spouse, is that it? He's being attended to, we're doctors, interns, he's going to be at University Hospital in about two shakes..."

Beyond his shoulder she could see another white-clad man and a city policeman carrying a form strapped to a stretcher out the door—she caught a flash of spun-brass hair at the stretcher's end just before it disappeared.

Then what had happened just before she had fainted came back: the sunlight spilling through the venetian blinds painting all with orange fire as acrid tendrils of gunsmoke twisted lazily in the air, herself and Randy across from one another over the prostrate gasping Miller, she keeping her eyes from the ghastly purple but nearly bloodless hole high on Miller's left pectoral until it disappeared beneath the dampened towel Randy placed over it. Miller's breathing was harsh and phlegmy but his eyes were open and his jaws worked as if he were trying to tell her something, not something of his pain, but something important she needed to know; she bent closer, her hair touching his sweat-pebbled brow, his brass-colored hair sticky-looking and matted with sweat; even as she bent closer some other part of her was grateful to Randy for being good in a crisis, for no sooner had the gun discharged and

204

Miller fallen than he'd been in the bathroom for towels, arranging some beneath Miller's head, then phoning the police, "There's been an accident, a person's been shot..."

She bent closer, some of her hair fell into Miller's eyes and she brushed it away: "Rings...rings...", Miller said, then: "Thayer...thay-er..." Did he mean "their"? Their what?

His eyes were shiny but not with tears. Her tears fell onto his face, mingling with his sweat and he rolled his head restlessly to one side. She was almost close enough to kiss him when he opened his mouth and out came a huge red sphere of blood and mucous, as if he were an aspirant in some obscene bubblegum contest. It grew bigger and bigger until it burst and a tiny spray touched her lips. She fainted.

*

She looked for the first time at the face of the black-haired man attending her. It was round and smooth and kindly; he was large and bulky and his clean hands seemed rather small. His light blue eyes seemed filled with concern: "Well, we're heading out to the hospital," he said. "I'm sorry this...is such a tough situation, not much I can say except, be brave—ah. Here's comes Paul."

The policeman had come back into the living room.

Lindsay clung to the intern's hand: "How is he? Oh, don't go. God. I just can't stand this!"

"Be brave—beareth all things, as the phrase goes. Sure you can stand it. The injured party's vital signs were still good but we have to go, there's not a second to waste." He squeezed her hand and was gone.

"Miss?" The policeman squatted beside her chair and put his hand on the overstuffed arm. He was young, too, like the emergency man, a little older than she was, maybe, and just a little younger, probably, than Miller. Without his uniform and other paraphanalia he might be just another nice moon-faced country boy working his way through college selling encyclopedias. Or a med or law student or whatever. "I'm officer Thomas Conroy. How are you feeling?"

Outside a siren groaned once but then didn't continue; she could hear what was no doubt the ambulance pulling away.

"Okay," she said. "Where's Randy?"

"That's the young fellow who had the weapon in his possession when the shooting occurred?"

"Yes."

"Well, he's down in the cruiser with my partner right now. And now we'd like for you both to come down to the station with us and see if we can't sort this thing out and determine the facts in the matter. Okay?"

"Yes, but what about Miller?"

"The University Hospital emergency treatment is just excellent—there isn't a place in the world he could get better emergency life-saving treatment. We'll check with them a little later after we get downtown.Want to try standing up?"

"Sure." She gripped his arm and got shakily up from the chair. "Can I ask you a favor?"

"What's that?"

"Can't we please just stop by at the hospital—Miller's my husband, please, I just can't stand not knowing. Please. I'm happy to go with you wherever and tell you whatever but please I have know about Miller. Please."

"Hmmmm. I shouldn't," he said.

"Please."

He sighed. "Maybe I can justify it this way: I guess we could swing down Muscatine and come by the U hospital first while we're on the way to the station, and you and I could make a quick trip in...but listen, if there's nothing to be learned yet, which may well be the case, then we'll all go right down to the station and start to, uh, get to the facts...you promise you'll abide by that?"

"Yes. Thank you."

They moved slowly to the door and then both stopped and looked back once around the living room: the ruined sofa, the litter on the coffee table and floor, the block of wood in the fireplace, the other sorry dreck of Miller's anguish.

For some reason she turned to the window to the left of the front door and reached for the cord to the blinds, intending to close them; just as her hand touched the cord a hideous percussive snarl came from outside, then stopped abruptly with a coughing sound, so startling her that she jumped as if she'd received an electric shock. She pulled the cord to further open the blinds and looked out upon Center Avenue. A police cruiser was parked in front of their house but the sun was glancing off it in such a way that she couldn't see the occupants.

206

Then the sunlight dimmed and the world went greenish and she hoped it would rain, not an electrical storm rain like you so often got in Iowa but a cooling, pure, ordinary rain.

She felt the young officer's hand warm on her elbow.

Then Lindsay heard it again: there was a sudden frightful coughing racket, then the mechanical snarl started up again, accelerated, and mounted to an ear-splitting pitch: peering through the slats of the blinds she could see the two city men with the chainsaw she'd noticed when she and Randy had driven up this afternoon. They were beginning to cut down a Dutch elm two houses down, and would no doubt soon arrive for the one before the Springstead home.

About the Author

Geoffrey Clark grew up in Michigan and attended Central Michigan University and the writer's workshop at the University of Iowa. He currently teaches writing at Roger Williams University in Rhode Island. His two previous collections of short fiction, *What the Moon Said* and *Ruffian on the Stair*, were published in 1983 and 1988 by Story Press.